Changing Middle Schools

Nancy L. Ames
Edward Miller

Changing
Middle Schools

How to Make Schools Work
for Young Adolescents

Jossey-Bass Publishers
San Francisco

Substantial discounts on bulk quantities of Jossey-Bass books are available to corporations, professional associations, and other organizations. For details and discount information, contact the special sales department at Jossey-Bass Inc., Publishers. (415) 433–1740; Fax (415) 433–0499.

For sales outside the United States, please contact your local Paramount Publishing International Office.

Manufactured in the United States of America. Nearly all Jossey-Bass books and jackets are printed on recycled paper that contains at least 50 percent recycled waste, including 10 percent postconsumer waste. Many of our materials are printed with either soy- or vegetable-based ink; during the printing process these inks emit fewer volatile organic compounds (VOCs) than petroleum-based inks. VOCs contribute to the formation of smog.

Library of Congress Cataloging-in-Publication Data

Ames, Nancy L., [date]
    Changing middle schools : how to make schools work for young adolescents / Nancy L. Ames, Edward Miller. — 1st ed.
      p. cm. — (The Jossey-Bass education series)
    Includes bibliographical references and index.
    ISBN 0-7879-0006-0
    1. Middle schools—United States—Case studies. 2. Education, Urban—United States—Case studies. 3. Educational change—United States—Case studies. I. Miller, Edward, [date]. II. Title. III. Series.
LB1623.5.U6A45   1994
373.2'36—dc20   94-22168
                                         CIP

FIRST EDITION
HB Printing   10 9 8 7 6 5 4 3 2 1   Code 94120

Contents

To the kids and those who care for them.

Preface

Brian is fourteen years old, intelligent, articulate, and living on the verge of tragedy. We met him at his middle school in one of Indiana's larger cities and spent a few days following him around to classes and talking to him about his life. We learned that, though he is classified as "gifted and talented," he is mainly bored with school, often in trouble with his teachers for goofing off and not paying attention, and generally considered lazy and "lacking social skills." He is one of those boys who sits in the back of the classroom, conspiring with a friend, making wisecracks, or simply lost in his own inner world. He talks fast, moves quickly, and frequently gets into fights. He carries a small hunting knife hidden in his jeans, just in case.

More than once Brian has come to school with bruises on his face and arms, and one of his teachers confides to us that she's sure he is regularly beaten at home. School officials reported the bruises to the child protection people once and there was an investigation, but nothing came of it—except that afterward Brian came to school with the worst black-and-blue marks yet. His teachers now see no point in filing further reports because, they say, they do not want to make things worse for him at home.

Brian likes reading, writing, and music, but schoolwork holds little interest for him, and he says there is no adult at school he can trust—no one he can talk to honestly about the things that really concern him. If things get really bad, he believes, there is no one he can count on to protect him except himself. With just a little prompting, he admits that it is his stepfather who hits him. His father abandoned the family when Brian was small. Things were not too bad for a while because his Uncle Jimmy was around to talk to him and do things with him. Then, a year ago, Uncle Jimmy was murdered. Now there is no one, and Brian's life is dominated by his fears and fantasies of violence and death.

Young adolescents, defined as children ages ten to fourteen, are living through some of the most important and drastic changes in the entire life cycle—changes in attachment, autonomy, sexuality, intimacy, achievement, and identity (Hill, 1980). During these years, schools play a critical role in helping young adolescents develop a positive self-image and the skills to deal with the enormous new emotional and social pressures they face. It is during these middle school years, grades five or six through eight, that the first indications of risky behavior and maladaptive patterns of school achievement often appear—patterns that may eventually lead to substance abuse, dropping out, premature sexual activity, and violence.

Brian's story above is real, though we have changed his name. His problems may be worse than those of most youngsters his age, but his situation is hardly unique. A great many urban children like Brian are affected by the poverty, violence, and crumbling social support network around them. They bring to school powerful feelings of anger, helplessness, and despair. Young adolescents in our cities pose a difficult challenge for middle-level educators, many of whom cling to traditional ideas of schooling that are ill suited to meet either the demands of our highly technological society or the profound human needs of the youngsters in their care. Moreover, school systems have historically done a poor job of focusing on the critical challenge of the middle grades. In the words of one commentator, "The nation's middle schools have long been treated as middle children often are, overlooked while attention is directed to the needs of their older counterparts, the high schools, and their younger ones, the elementary grades" (Celis, 1992).

How can Brian reach his full potential academically if his social and emotional needs are not met? It takes committed, talented educators and supportive school environments to ensure that neglected or abused children have a chance to succeed. *Changing Middle Schools* is the story of how a group of middle school educators, with the help of enlightened people in their local communities, are creating such supportive schools. The message of this book is compelling and urgent: remaking poor urban schools into places of hope and opportunity is essential—and *it can be done,* against all odds. Though access to the right resources is important, improving middle schools does not require staggering sums of money. Rather, it requires leadership, vision, and a culture of change.

The profound changes described in this book grew out of a deep personal commitment from teachers, principals, and support staff— a willingness to accept responsibility, individually and as a faculty, for the health and well-being of the young lives in their charge, and a willingness to reach out to the local community to obtain needed support. It is not just "a job" that the adults in these schools have undertaken. It is an act of conscience, born of a moral imperative to value each child as a whole person deserving of love, respect, and an equal opportunity to learn.

While high moral purpose is a prerequisite for the kind of profound change we describe, it alone is not enough. As Michael Fullan has observed, moral purpose without the skills to nurture and manage school change will inevitably produce martyrdom and burnout. Those essential skills are today being developed and refined by innovative, reflective middle school educators across the United States. Our goal is to contribute to the growing literature of their struggles and successes by offering a rich portrait of some of their most exemplary efforts.

The Origins of This Book

Changing Middle Schools tells the stories of four urban middle schools that have undergone deep transformation. All are part of the Middle Grades Improvement Program, affectionately known as MGIP ("em-gip")—one of the first and most ambitious of the current efforts at systemic middle school reform. For nearly seven years MGIP has nurtured fundamental changes in school climate and structure and classroom practice in sixteen urban school districts comprising sixty-five schools across the state of Indiana.

MGIP was the brainchild of Joan Lipsitz, a longtime champion of middle-level education and the 1993 recipient of the National Middle School Association's Lounsbury Award. In her first book, *Growing Up Forgotten* (1977), Lipsitz writes about the needs of young adolescents and the concept of a school grounded in the realities of human development and the related principles of teaching and learning. A year later she founded the Center for Early Adolescence at the University of North Carolina. In *Successful Schools for Young Adolescents* (1984), Lipsitz provides vivid models for those attempting to embark on middle school reform.

Lipsitz launched MGIP in late 1986 after moving to Lilly Endowment Inc. (hereafter called the Lilly Endowment or the endowment) in Indianapolis. Her ultimate goal was to bring about fundamental change in urban school systems throughout Indiana, but she chose to focus first on the middle grades, not just because they were her long-standing passion but also because data suggested that the number of students who fail in school, particularly in poor and minority communities, increased steadily from fifth through eighth or ninth grade.

As another observer pointed out, Indiana was "an unlikely setting for a middle grades renaissance" (Mancini, 1993, p. v). In 1986 its urban middle schools, from Indianapolis to Fort Wayne to Terre Haute, exhibited all the classic symptoms of a national education system in crisis: students and teachers alienated from each other; violence; high rates of suspensions, expulsions, and absenteeism; low test scores; students with overwhelming social and emotional needs; and a general climate of disrespect for the teaching profession.

Like their counterparts in the rest of the country, Indiana's middle schools were "feeder" schools that prepared students for a carefully prescribed high school experience. Many middle school teachers had been trained simply as "secondary" teachers, and significant numbers of them neither understood the particular needs of young adolescents nor relished the idea of working with them. Furthermore, there was little impetus for change at the state level or among Indiana's universities or professional teachers' associations. Into this picture stepped the endowment, intent on changing the very nature of the participating schools—structure, curriculum and instruction, and the relationships between teachers and children.

The endowment believed that such a transformation could happen only with the support of local schools and communities. For school systems to "buy in" to the reforms, they would have to be full partners in the design of the changes to come. Thus the endowment began by asking districts to submit planning proposals. The ensuing planning grants ranged from $15,000 to $25,000 and lasted from six months to a year. They helped foster local planning and reflection, creativity and risk taking, and broad participation of both school and community members in the program design.

After the planning was completed, the endowment provided discretionary funds—up to $150,000 over a three-year period—to those school districts whose implementation proposals demonstrated a strong commitment to bringing about fundamental change. The endowment had no preestablished vision; it encouraged "bottom-up" change tailored to local needs and conditions. Districts could use their funds in a variety of ways: for information gathering, staff development, conference attendance, site visits, meetings, consultants, new programs, student incentives, and so on.

The shape of reform was not left entirely to the individual district design teams. The endowment encouraged participating schools to begin by examining their existing programs in light of the developmental needs of young adolescents, and it also advised them to focus first on school organization and climate rather than on curriculum and instruction. "Until the schools became deeply thoughtful about the developmental stage that these kids are in and deeply thoughtful about their homes, communities, and the climate in the school itself," said Lipsitz, "a change in math texts or instructional techniques would have been as much of a disappointment as it had always been."

The endowment also wanted local efforts to be guided by the latest research and best practice. Therefore, it offered participating districts the help of skilled technical assistance consultants in preparing their proposals and implementing their reform efforts. To this day, these consultants remain an integral component of the program.

Over the years, the endowment added several strategies to its original program design in response to changing needs and conditions. Interested readers will find a complete description of the MGIP initiative as it evolved over time in the Appendix. Four of these strategies, however, are of particular importance.

First, the endowment offered another round of grants to those school systems whose initial three-year implementation grants had expired. These "Phase II" grants required school systems to tighten and focus their school improvement efforts. The endowment also laid out three "nonnegotiables" designed to reduce or eliminate three harmful practices: rigid tracking of students by academic ability, corporal punishment, and suspension and expulsion as discipline measures.

Second, the endowment introduced a minigrant program to "deepen the instructional process" by encouraging teacher creativity and fostering connections across the disciplines. These MGIP-X grants (the "X" for "extension") were in the range of $7,500 to $15,000. The endowment sponsored several rounds of minigrants, each of which aimed at linking different disciplines: (1) reading, writing, and language arts; (2) social studies and the arts; and (3) science, mathematics, and related technology.

Third, the endowment engaged Education Development Center (EDC), a nonprofit research and development firm with thirty years of experience in school reform work, to help improve curriculum and instruction in the participating sites.

Fourth, and perhaps most important, the endowment created the MGIP Network in 1989 to link the participating sites. According to Director Barbara Jackson, the network's goal was to "reduce isolation on the part of individual teachers and school systems and foster common interests while preserving local autonomy and control." The network sets direction, provides sites with information, sponsors joint professional development activities, promotes collaboration among the sites, and administers its own minigrant program as a catalyst for change. It also collaborates with other state, regional, and national organizations to improve programs and services for young adolescents.

In *Gentle Ambitions: Indiana's Thoughtful Middle Grades Movement*, Gail Mancini describes the tremendous change that has occurred in Indiana middle schools. "The very fact that the middle level movement plows ahead despite obstacles is what makes Indiana such an interesting case. In the scope of the entire country, few state or local leaders have taken a systematic approach to creating exemplary middle schools. . . . Indiana's movement thrives backstage—slowly, often unnoticed" (1993, p. vii). We hope that, with the publication of this book, others will begin to take notice.

The Purpose of This Book

There are 8,272 middle schools and 4,512 junior high schools in the United States, employing about 30,000 administrators, 30,000 counselors and other support staff, and 360,000 teachers. Many of these practitioners are already engaged in or about to initiate the kinds of school change described in these pages. Federal and state policy and grant makers as well as private foundations interested in supporting local school reform efforts are also increasingly turning their attention to the middle grades.

Among the most frequently asked questions of these practitioners, policy makers, and funders are the following: What can we learn from the experiences of schools in an intensive reform effort like MGIP? What do successful urban middle schools look like? How can resource-hungry urban schools achieve this vision? What is the role of middle school principals, central office administrators, teachers, parents, and community members in the change effort? In what ways can outside funders and policy makers help bring about systemic school reform?

Changing Middle Schools has two central objectives. The first is to inspire—to contribute to that essential sense of high moral purpose in school reform by painting an intimate portrait of the changes that took place in four carefully selected MGIP schools. We chose to spotlight individual schools because, while MGIP's goal was systemic reform, actual changes occurred primarily at the building level. Where the central office led the reform effort by changing local policies, providing additional staff and resources, or offering technical support, we describe its role. At many of the MGIP sites, however, the central office was a minor player—at best, following rather than leading individual schools' efforts; at worst, getting in the way.

Through these school portraits we hope to move beyond education jargon and give readers a true picture of reform in practice, with a richness of description that captures the complexity of real life in schools and the clash of new ideas with established ways of schooling. The reality of life in schools is not ultimately about policies, structures, and curricula but about people and their relationships to each other. Thus we have tried to tell these schools' stories in the words of the people living them—administrators, teachers, students, parents, support staff, and community members.

It is important to point out that *Changing Middle Schools* is not an evaluation, nor is it based on hard research data or statistical analyses. The four schools highlighted were each nominated by those close to the program: one or more technical assistance consultants, Lilly Endowment staff, or others working to bring about middle-level reform in Indiana. We visited more than ten MGIP schools prior to making our selections, and virtually all of them were worthy of inclusion in this book. We ultimately chose these four not only because they had made considerable progress but also because they had taken different paths on the road to reform.

To prepare these portraits each of us spent several days at each school observing classrooms; attending team meetings; and interviewing dozens of administrators, teachers, parents, students, and support staff. In each school we chose to "shadow" one or more students to experience a typical school day from their perspective. We also reviewed school records and documents describing the school philosophy, policies, practices, and outcomes. With the exception of Billy Bones and David Born in Chapter Two and the student poets in Chapter Three, the names of all students have been changed.

No single school described in this study has succeeded on every front. Indeed, each continues to struggle with critical issues like discipline policy, curriculum and instruction, equity, and sensitivity to cultural differences. Yet each has won significant battles. The evidence of victory includes rising student achievement, higher attendance, less violence and vandalism, growing parental and community support, and a vast improvement in staff morale. Together, these schools tell an inspiring story of expanding opportunity for children on the very margins of the public education system in the United States.

The second objective of *Changing Middle Schools* is to help readers understand better some of the specific issues involved in middle school restructuring, and thus to help them develop the essential skills for nurturing school change. Nine principles are central to our findings:

1. Changing middle schools begins with personalizing adult-child relationships. Reaching the child's mind begins with reaching his or her heart.

2. Changing middle schools requires personalizing adult relationships. School structures must support collaboration and

shared decision making; teachers must enter into a true community of learning and practice.

3. Changing middle schools requires transformational leadership. Transformational leaders have a clear vision; are themselves eager learners; take risks; share decision making; are entrepreneurial; and are accessible to staff, parents, and students alike.

4. Changing middle schools requires both careful planning and ongoing reflection. Data are used to drive decisions, and new policies and practices are evaluated and revised based on the results.

5. Changing middle schools requires comprehensive restructuring, not just tinkering at the edges. Restructuring begins with changes in roles and relationships and develops through changes in school organization and scheduling, curriculum and instruction, student support services, and professional development.

6. Changing middle schools requires establishing close links among home, school, and community. Schools reach out to parents and community members for support, while parents and community members also reach in.

7. District-level support is helpful but not essential for change in individual schools and classrooms. For change to occur across multiple schools and multiple classrooms, however, it may be a prerequisite.

8. Changing middle schools requires both external and internal change agents. External change agents have an important role to play as advisers, cheerleaders, and critical friends, while internal change agents make things happen from within.

9. Changing middle schools requires a multifaceted intervention strategy. The seeds of change must be planted and cultivated over a reasonable span of time and geared to the needs and strengths of each school's students and staff.

Ultimately, we hope that *Changing Middle Schools* will provide its readers with clues regarding the evolutionary change process and the tensions and struggles that inevitably accompany deep, enduring change. At the same time, this book is not a prescription for school reform or a how-to manual. There is no one route for successful school change. Those who embark on the journey must chart their own courses—exploring, experimenting, reflecting, and, above all, feeling. What *Changing Middle Schools* offers is a compass to help point the way.

Who Should Read This Book

Numerous books on middle-level education have been published in recent years; none has described in detail the complex, systemic nature of sustained school change. We believe that these detailed portraits of schools in the midst of transformation will be especially useful to a wide audience of middle school administrators, teachers, support staff, consultants, researchers, policy makers, curriculum designers, and parents.

Principals will find a vision of successful middle schools, along with insights about the nature of the change process. They will discover what it means to be a "transformational leader" and learn how others have dealt with a host of practical problems associated with moving from a traditional junior high school to an effective middle school.

Teachers will find rich descriptions of teaming—the process, the benefits, and the pitfalls—and student advisory programs, interdisciplinary instruction, and innovative teaching strategies. They will also find compelling portraits of real-life role models—the dedicated middle school teachers who are the true heroes and heroines of these stories.

Guidance counselors, school psychologists, social workers, school nurses, and other support staff will read about student assistance programs that provide young adolescents with an array of health, mental health, and social services. They will also learn about ways of involving other agencies in the community in providing comprehensive school-linked services.

Changing Middle Schools also offers state and local policy makers (superintendents, school board members, legislators), as well as parent and community activists, a vision of effective middle-level education and a greater understanding of the ways in which they can help schools achieve this vision. Finally, the book provides teachers and students in teachers' colleges and schools of education with authentic, readable portraits of schools in the midst of fundamental reform.

The Organization of the Book

Chapter One describes the unique developmental needs of young adolescents and introduces the concept of "personalization" as a way of meeting those needs. Personalization encompasses six key elements: (1) understanding the developmental challenges of early adolescence; (2) valuing and respecting each student; (3) developing close adult-child relationships; (4) designing and implementing developmentally appropriate curricula and instruction that are sensitive to individual differences; (5) providing a range of health, mental health, and social services to meet students' needs; and (6) building strong links among family, school, and community.

Chapter Two takes readers on a tour of Sarah Scott, a little school in the poorest part of the city that has succeeded in turning itself around by creating a caring, familylike atmosphere. The motto of the school is "Everybody Is Somebody," and the faculty at Sarah Scott works hard to make that slogan a reality. Sarah Scott illustrates the critical importance of close personal relationships—relationships between adults and students, principal and staff, staff and parents. Through the regular curriculum, field visits, career exploration programs, and community partnerships, teachers at

Sarah Scott help students expand their horizons and their vision of their possible selves.

Chapter Three shows how Harshman Middle School, an inner-city school that serves what may be the highest-risk population in the state, is addressing the overwhelming social, emotional, physical, and educational needs of its students. In this case, we find an experienced, capable principal, Marcia Capuano, with a strong devotion to young adolescents and boundless energy. A quiet leader, Capuano had a vision for her school, set clear priorities, and within three years had achieved some stunning successes.

Recognizing that students could not learn unless their basic needs were met, Capuano created an on-site health clinic and provided students with a comprehensive array of psychological and social services. At the same time, she took steps to strengthen the school's academic program, beginning with reading and language arts. To enlist parent and community support, she initiated several programs designed to link Harshman with the surrounding community.

The next two chapters focus on Decatur Middle School, one of the pioneers in the Middle Grades Improvement Program. Located just outside Indianapolis, Decatur Township is primarily a blue-collar community; 12 percent of its middle school students are African American, bused in each day from a poor neighborhood on the other side of the city.

In Chapter Four, readers meet five teachers at Decatur Middle School who exemplify the best in interdisciplinary teaming. This chapter illustrates how teaming can support various aspects of personalization: a belief in and high expectations for students; close interpersonal relationships; and rich curricula and instruction that are active, thought-provoking, and relevant to young adolescents' interests and concerns. Above all, the teachers on Team 8C are willing to share their innermost thoughts and feelings in order to reach their students, especially those that are most fragile and in need of adult love and support.

In Chapter Five, readers find a portrait of the two principals—Jeff Swensson and Wally Bourke—who helped transform Decatur Middle School from a relatively unfocused, traditional junior high school to a modern middle school with clear priorities. Both are charismatic leaders who have gone on to positions of leadership in the Indiana middle school movement. Their story, and its post-script, suggests that it is possible to have smooth transitions in leadership if those leaders share a common vision.

Chapter Six illustrates how strong central office support can play a major role in bringing about change not just in one isolated school but across all the schools in a large urban system. In this case, readers meet Sandy Todd, the district's MGIP coordinator, and Judy Johnston, the technical assistance consultant provided by the endowment, who both played a major role in bringing about change across Fort Wayne's eleven middle schools.

This chapter focuses especially on Portage Middle School, a relative newcomer to the middle school reform movement, which made significant advances in two short years. Portage personalized its program in a number of ways—for example, by eliminating tracking, including students with disabilities in the regular education program, and creating preventive guidance programs.

Finally, Chapter Seven summarizes the implications of the Middle Grades Improvement Program for those seeking to bring about systemic school reform. It describes the roles of principals, central office staff, external change agents, and discretionary funds in bringing about school restructuring, and argues that personalizing middle schools begins with changing adult relationships. Systemic school change also benefits from personal efforts on the part of program sponsors and change agents.

The appendix contains a more complete description of the MGIP initiative, including its underlying philosophy and goals, key features of the original design, and changes made by the Lilly Endowment over time. Policy makers and program sponsors will find the endowment's multifaceted and highly personalized approach to statewide reform instructive. After it awarded relatively open-ended planning and implementation grants to the participating school systems, the endowment introduced a number of carrots, sticks, and support systems to help bring about desired changes in participating schools and classrooms.

Acknowledgments

We wish to thank the Lilly Endowment, and especially Joan Lipsitz, for making this book possible. From the beginning, Joan helped conceptualize the book and give it life. Her own work served as an inspiration throughout, and her tough and thoughtful review helped sharpen the book as it unfolded.

We are indebted to all those who gave their time to meet with us and were willing to share their accomplishments together with their hard-won lessons. They opened not only their schools and classrooms to us, but also their hearts.

We also wish to thank our colleagues at EDC, especially Janet Whitla, Judith Zorfass, Catherine Cobb Morocco, and Sharon Grollman for their thoughtful reviews. Jeanne Knox provided capable developmental editing of selected chapters, Sookim Rosch spent many hours producing and distributing draft copies and obtaining releases, Shira Persky helped gather background material and check references, and Eliza Miller ably transcribed tape-recorded interviews.

We are indebted to Ted Sizer, Jim Comer, Howard Gardner, Mindy Kornhaber, Norris Haynes, and other members of the ATLAS Communities Seminar. Their writings and ongoing conversations about the concept of personalization helped frame the book's theme. We have drawn liberally from these conversations in the first chapter.

We are also grateful to Lesley Iura, our editor at Jossey-Bass Publishers, without whose encouragement and support this book would not have been possible.

Finally, to our families and loved ones, who put up with us during the lengthy writing process: our humble thanks for the many nights and weekends that you were willing to take second place to our elusive muse.

August 1994   Nancy L. Ames
                                                 Newton, Massachusetts

                                                 Edward Miller
                                                 Cambridge, Massachusetts

The Authors

Nancy L. Ames is vice president and director of Family, School, and Community Programs at Education Development Center, Inc. (EDC), a nonprofit research and development organization dedicated to human development through education. She has designed and monitored a wide range of projects aimed at improving classroom instruction, enhancing teacher growth and development, and promoting school reform. Ames received a bachelor of science degree from Tufts University in 1966, where she majored in psychology. She received a master's degree in education from Fresno State University in 1970.

Ames began her career with the Developmental Research Division of the Educational Testing Service in 1967. Later, she served as a research and evaluation consultant for the Fresno City School System and the California State Department of Education. As senior analyst at Abt Associates Inc., Ames conducted a variety of policy research studies, with a particular emphasis on improving education for children at risk. Since joining EDC, she has focused her attention on large-scale systemic change efforts such as the ATLAS Communities project, a collaborative effort of EDC, the Coalition of Essential Schools at Brown University, the School Development Program at Yale University, and Harvard University's Project Zero to "break the mold" of U.S. education.

Ames has published articles and research reports and given presentations on topics encompassing early childhood education, compensatory education, vocational education, special education, school safety, and school restructuring. She has authored two books:

Sex Fairness in Career Guidance: A Learning Kit (1975) and *Who Benefits from Federal Education Dollars: The Development of ESEA Title I Policy* (1980).

For the last six years, Ames has been following the progress of the Middle Grades Improvement Program in Indiana. She witnessed the early stages of program implementation, helped launch the MGIP Network, attended numerous MGIP planning sessions, participated in seminal events, and met with dozens of administrators and teachers over the life of the project. The program's unofficial historian and recorder, she has kept close track of its accomplishments as they have evolved over time.

Edward Miller is editor of the *Harvard Education Letter*, published at the Harvard Graduate School of Education. Both his A.B. degree (1973) in music theory and composition and his Ed.M. degree (1992) are from Harvard. He was the founding editor of *Highwire: The National Student Magazine* and edited *Earthwatch* magazine and the *Harvard* [Mass.] *Post*, a small-town weekly newspaper. For eight years he taught expository writing at Harvard College (a course he himself had failed as a freshman).

Miller has published articles on a wide range of education issues, including motivation, grades, national standards, scheduling, and school food. His case study of peer sexual harassment in high school, entitled "Lisa's Complaint," will appear in 1995 in Judith Kleinfeld's book *Gender Wars*. He is coauthor, with Kathleen Cushman and Larry Anderson, of *How to Produce a Small Newspaper: A Guide for Independent Journalists* (1983). He received the Distinguished Achievement Award of the Educational Press Association of America in 1994 for his work on the *Harvard Education Letter* and was nominated for two National Magazine Awards in 1983 for *Highwire*. In 1987 he won the Bedford Prize, given by St. Martin's Press, for outstanding teaching of writing at the college level.

Miller is chairman of the board of trustees of Opus 118 Music Center, a nonprofit corporation that provides instrumental music instruction to public school children in East Harlem, New York City, and also serves as an adviser to the Boston Music Education Collaborative. He plays the viola, but not particularly well.

Changing Middle Schools

Chapter One

Personalizing Middle Schools

Walk into Sarah Scott Middle School in Terre Haute, Indiana, one day and into H. L. Harshman Middle School in Indianapolis the next, and you will be struck by the contrast. Both schools have participated in Indiana's Middle Grades Improvement Program (MGIP) over the past several years, and both have undergone enormous changes during that time. Both are, in many ways, exemplary schools. Yet superficially they look and feel very different.

Sarah Scott is a small school in a stately old building, and though Terre Haute is a fair-sized city, the feeling you get on entering is that you have walked into a small town where everyone knows everyone else. The old-fashioned high-ceilinged corridors and stairwells are swept clean and the walls are covered with neatly arrayed posters and displays. Adults and children alike smile at you, greet you, and ask if they can help you find your way.

The look and feel of the Harshman School is anything but small-town. This is the big city, and its face is harder and tougher. Indeed, Harshman is in the heart of one of the most depressed areas of Indianapolis. The low-ceilinged, blocklike 1950s style of the building contributes to the crowded, noisy feeling in the halls. More than half the students at Harshman are black, and almost all are poor. The banter and bumping in the corridors when classes are changing have a decidedly urban edge to them.

The contrast between these two schools mirrors the experience of middle school students themselves as they enter adolescence. Nothing is so striking about young adolescents as their superficial differences from each other, even at the same chronological age and grade level.

The years from age ten to age fourteen are among the most turbulent in the human life span. Within a relatively short period, young adolescents experience profound changes in physical, intellectual, social, and emotional development. They experiment with new social roles; must deal with their rapidly changing, often unrecognizable, bodies; and face new expectations from the world around them (Mitchell, 1979). Over the past fifteen years researchers and educators have defined and described a comprehensive middle-level educational philosophy based on the unique needs of ten- to fourteen-year-olds. This philosophy, which was the foundation of the Lilly Endowment's MGIP initiative, starts with the premise that effective middle school teachers and administrators must understand and value young adolescents as human beings. Foremost among their unique needs is the need to be known, heard, and respected as an individual.

We visited a variety of urban middle schools in the midst of change and growth in our research for this book. The four schools we ultimately chose to write about in detail were superficially very different from each other, yet they were alike in one crucial way. Each had made enormous progress in transforming itself into an effective school through deeply held beliefs about the innate worth and dignity of every child, and by making a profound commitment to personalizing the experience of school for young adolescents.

What do we mean by personalizing the middle school experience? We believe that personalization

- Begins with a deep understanding of the developmental challenges of early adolescence
- Requires valuing and respecting each student, regardless of race, ethnicity, socioeconomic status, gender, or disability
- Involves close adult-child relationships that facilitate the transition from childhood to adulthood

- Demands rich, developmentally appropriate curricula and instruction that are sensitive to individual differences
- Calls for a range of support services that address students' social, emotional, and physical needs as well as their academic development
- Involves building strong links among family, school, and community so that all work in harmony to support children's development

Moreover, we discovered that personalization was not only the key to effective middle schools but also the underlying theme common to each of these schools' stories of how they were able to manage the process of change itself. Just as there is no one style of teaching or learning that is appropriate for every student, there is no one template for change that fits every school. Perhaps the most valuable lesson of the MGIP story is the way in which this systemic reform initiative managed to build into its design the room for individual schools to find their own unique paths to growth and transformation, based on the particular needs of their own students and staffs.

Understanding Young Adolescents

Joan Lipsitz argues that successful middle schools begin with an understanding of the "why" of middle-level education—the developmental challenges that young adolescents face as they move from childhood to adulthood. Without that understanding, educators cannot possibly deal with the "what" and "how" of schooling.

Many middle-level educators have now come to recognize that early adolescence is a time of dramatic and sometimes traumatic changes. The physical changes are most obvious. Young adolescents grow an average of two to four inches and gain eight to ten pounds per year during this period. As their bodies shoot upward, their feet and hands grow too big, their arms too long. Hands dangle from suddenly too-short sleeves; socks peek out from pants that were the right length just a few weeks ago.

Physical growth occurs unevenly, and thus certain parts of the body—notably hands, feet, ears, and noses—often develop earlier and more rapidly. Clumsy and not yet comfortable with their new bodies, boys especially are apt to trip over their own feet, bump into things, and knock things over at the kitchen table or in the lunchroom. These physical changes significantly alter the way young adolescents see and think about themselves. Insecure about their relationships with peers and their worth as individuals, they worry incessantly about their appearance and spend endless hours peering into mirrors, arranging their hair, and applying acne medicines.

The hormones that play havoc with complexions during this period are also bringing on confusing physical changes and powerful sexual feelings for both girls and boys. Since the age of onset of puberty varies tremendously among both girls and boys, it is entirely normal for one thirteen-year-old to appear completely physically mature, while another still looks like a young child. Newly discovered sexual feelings engender greater interest in and anxiety about the opposite sex. Some girls welcome the changes in their bodies and are eager to show off their new adult figures by wearing tight sweaters and miniskirts. Others wear baggy sweaters and loose-fitting pants in an attempt to hide all outward signs of their emerging sexuality. Although some boys carry their new manhood proudly, others are ashamed of their gangly appearance, hirsute faces, and cracking voices. Hunched over, hands in pockets, they avoid looking you in the eye and may seem unable to speak.

Yet these physical and sexual developments are just the most obvious of the changes youngsters experience at this stage of life. Young adolescents are also changing cognitively, socially, and emotionally. They know that they must soon put away "childish things" (as adults are apt to advise them), and yet a great many young adolescents are not quite ready to give up the safety and relative serenity of childhood. They are eager to loosen the bonds to parents, but they have not yet developed new, more mature patterns of relationship. And they have neither the skills nor the confidence to become fully autonomous.

It is not surprising, then, for young adolescents to feel waves of anger, excitement, anxiety, depression, and other emotions as they experiment with more adult behaviors. Caught between childhood and adulthood, they seem to change from one moment to the next—alternately independent, immature, energized, lethargic, sensitive, oblivious, eager, confused, responsible, and disorganized.

The traditional junior high school, as many other observers have pointed out, is ill equipped to deal with the challenge of working with young adolescents. Many such schools were designed to imitate the impersonal structure and atmosphere of senior high schools, with students moving from class to class, teacher to teacher, in forty- or forty-five-minute periods. This approach drastically reduces the possibility that any one adult would come to know an individual student well enough to understand or have time to think about that student's inner turmoil and doubt.

Moreover, since junior high schools were traditionally classified as secondary rather than elementary schools, most junior high teachers were trained to teach high school, with a primary emphasis on their subject specialty—English, math, biology, social studies, and so on—rather than on the developmental needs of children. Many of these teachers viewed assignment to junior high classrooms as a second choice, or even as a punishment, and thus approached their work with a preconceived attitude of negativity and resentment. Some saw their time at the junior high level as something to be endured until they could get the job they really wanted and were trained to perform: teaching high school. Faced with young adolescents' chameleon-like behavior, it was not uncommon for such teachers to shake their heads in frustration or despair: "I don't know what to do with these kids." "They're so moody." "All they care about is the opposite sex." "They just can't keep still." "They'll be the death of me."

Enlightened educators, like those described in this book, now take a much more positive view of the middle school child. They see the child at the point of transition to adulthood as a source of wonder and meaning. Like Benson, Williams, and Johnson, they view early adolescence as a time when "one begins to catch a glimpse of the emerging adult side by side with the child, when leadership begins to make itself visible, when the capacity for abstract thought develops, and when, perhaps for the first time, a parent or teacher can hold a conversation with the young person that has the tone of adult to adult communication" (1987, p. 4).

Valuing and Respecting Each Student

In addition to understanding and attending to the developmental challenges faced by young adolescents as a group, these educators value and respect individual differences. They feel a responsibility to know each child's strengths and weaknesses, family and cultural background, interests, and learning style. And they use a variety of strategies to help all students feel cherished. Linda Darling-Hammond calls this focus on individual differences a critical feature of "learner-centered" schools: "Learner-centered schools focus on students' needs, interests and talents as the basis for organizing school work and school organization, building curriculum and learning opportunities, and developing relationships between and among students, educators and parents. Such schools are by definition grounded in an appreciation and deep valuing of human diversity. They are rooted in our diverse human experiences, and they open up the infinite reaches of human possibility" (1992, p. 19).

Implicit in this description of learner-centered or personalized schools are two interrelated concepts: (1) setting high expectations and providing opportunities for success to all students, while (2) attending to the diversity among them.

Giving all students a meaningful chance to succeed is one of the basic recommendations of *Turning Points*, the Carnegie Corporation on Adolescent Development's report on middle-level education: "All young adolescents should have the opportunity to succeed in every aspect of the middle grade program, regardless of previous achievement or the pace at which they learn" (1990, p. 14). By offering *all* students the opportunity to participate in advanced courses, exploratory programs, and extracurricular activities, successful middle schools communicate to both youngsters and their parents that *all* children have value.

Despite this recommendation, tracking students by achievement level remains an almost universal practice in today's middle schools. In theory, tracking allows teachers to tailor instruction to each group's knowledge and skills and thus supports individualized instruction. In practice, lower tracks often focus on boring, repetitive basic-skills drills. There is little evidence that tracking benefits those in the lower tracks (or that heterogeneous grouping hurts those in the upper tracks). On the contrary, tracking has a negative impact on low-achieving students' aspirations and self-esteem, while denying them access to the advanced courses they need to get into college and find rewarding careers (Oakes, 1985; Wheelock, 1992).

Personalized middle schools recognize that all students can benefit greatly from participation in challenging and exciting school projects and from rich, thought-provoking curricula (Epstein, 1988; Lipsitz, 1984; Levin, 1987; Wheelock and Dorman, 1988). The strategies for making success possible for all learners include cooperative learning groups, cross-age tutors, specially designed curricula, and other support services.

Valuing and respecting young adolescents also means attending to cultural differences. The demographic map of American society is changing dramatically, because of both immigration and higher birth rates among racial and ethnic minority populations. In 1980, minority youth made up 15 percent of the school-age population. It is expected to reach 50 percent by the year 2020. A disproportionate number of these youth live in poor urban centers, where unemployment, racial tension, and violence abound. Meanwhile, city and state budgets for public schools and youth services are stretched to the breaking point.

In 1989, the Carnegie Corporation issued the following warning: "The specter of a divided society—one affluent and the other poor—looms ominously on the American horizon. Inherent in this scenario is the potential for serious conflict between generations, among races and ethnic groups, and between the economically disenfranchised and middle- and upper-income groups. It is a disturbing scenario which must not occur" (p. 32).

One way to help avoid this scenario is for urban schools to understand and give value to children's differing cultural backgrounds. Schools must acknowledge racial and cultural tensions and face them head on. They must work hard to "provide culturally sensitive and validating experiences to students from many different cultural backgrounds" (Haynes, 1994, p. 14). They must aim to expand their students' conception of what it means to be human in a culturally diverse world and to develop cross-cultural competency (Boateng, 1990). In addition, they must be willing to examine their own policies and practices to see whether they are influenced by racial, ethnic, gender, and socioeconomic stereotypes.

The Holmes Group summed up this imperative for personalized middle schools well: "When teachers learn more about their students they can build learning communities that embrace rather than smother cultural diversity. Students do differ. Without stereotyping or prepackaged responses, such differences can become opportunities for richer learning. . . . We speak of celebrating diversity because we believe that the hallmark of a true learning community is its inclusiveness—where teachers take the responsibility for helping each child take part to his or her fullest. The idea of a learning community has special significance in a democracy where all must find their voice" (1990, p. 35).

At Decatur Middle School, described later in this book, we witnessed the effects of such inclusiveness. We saw and heard how a black student, struggling to come to terms with historical racism and his own African-American identity, was touched, held, supported, and listened to by an exemplary team of teachers. These educators were motivated not only by the conviction that cultural differences must be attended to and valued but also by simple affection for the boy as a person and sympathy for his struggles as a young adolescent. "We just love him to death," they told us, speaking of a young man poised on the verge of drugs and violence, one whom too many traditional teachers would have seen simply as trouble.

Developing Close Adult-Child Relationships

Many middle school researchers and observers recognize the importance of establishing close personal connections between adults and the young adolescents in their charge. As Braddock and McPartland write, "Students must also be attached to their schools in human terms and on a personal level, with the perception that their teachers care about them as individuals and the belief that the professionals at their schools will actively support their efforts to learn" (1992, p. 160).

James Comer, director of the School Development Program at Yale University, believes that respectful, trusting personal relationships among children, teachers, principals, and parents are vital to creating an atmosphere in which children and learning thrive. "Learning isn't a mechanical process," Comer asserts. "Motivation and commitment to learning don't happen just by having somebody stand up and try to pump information into you. You have to work on making the school a place where people connect emotionally. If you don't do that, then you're not going to succeed" (1988, p. 5).

David Hawkins, a pioneer in the area of substance abuse prevention, also speaks of the critical importance of bonding between adults and young adolescents. According to Hawkins's research, those youngsters who successfully survived a multiple-risk environment had all bonded closely with someone who took an interest in them, who held out clear standards and expectations, and with whom they felt close emotionally. In his view, what we need now is not a "war on drugs" but a "war for bonding" (Hawkins, 1993).

Personalizing urban middle schools requires establishing close relationships between adults and children. But such relationships do not just happen by chance; the structure of the school must be designed to support such bonds.

For example, adviser-advisee programs aim at bringing adults into close relationships with students. The National Middle School Association (NMSA) advises that "each young learner needs an adult who knows him or her well and is in a position to give individual attention. Therefore, the middle school should be organized so that every youngster has such an adult, one who has special responsibility for the individual's academic and personal welfare. Home-base or adviser-advisee programs which provide individuals with regular opportunities for interaction with a small group of peers and a caring environment fill this need" (1982, p. 19).

Another structure that helps promote meaningful adult-child relationships is interdisciplinary teaming, in which a team of teachers is responsible for a community of students. Creating smaller communities for teaching and learning was one of the major recommendations of *Turning Points* (Carnegie Corporation, 1989). But smaller student-teacher ratios are not enough. As Theodore Sizer (1994) points out, colleagues must work with the identical group of kids and have time each day to talk about those kids and what "knowing them" means.

Transforming Curriculum and Instruction

Personalization does not end with understanding and valuing young adolescents or establishing close relationships with them. Middle school teachers must also re-examine and, if necessary, refocus what they teach, how they teach it, and how they measure the results. "Centering schools on learners influences how we think about curriculum and its connections to students' experiences, culture and personal meaning, how we think about assessment and its capacity to illuminate the full range of students' multiple intelligences and achievement, how we think about teaching and its responsiveness to students' conceptions and understandings" (Darling-Hammond, 1992, p. 19). At the middle level, personalization means designing curriculum and instruction to meet the needs of young adolescents, while attending to the tremendous variation within and among them.

Children first develop the ability to reason abstractly in early adolescence. "They begin to think of the world around them and themselves in new ways. For the first time, young adolescents can 'think about thinking'—which often confuses them. This 'reflexive thinking' allows them to form sophisticated self-concepts that are shaped by interactions between their experiences and new powers of reasoning" (Van Hoose and Strahan, 1988, p. 13).

Jean Piaget's stage theory of mental development describes early adolescence as roughly the age when youngsters move from "concrete operations" to "formal operations" (1977). Students in the concrete-operations stage, says Piaget, can solve mathematical or logical problems when faced with concrete situations in which they can see, touch, or manipulate objects. As they enter the formal-operations stage, they develop the ability to reason logically in the absence of concrete objects. They begin to understand and apply advanced mathematical and scientific concepts, and they reason on the basis of possibilities instead of being limited by their own direct experiences.

And yet, as with other characteristics of early adolescence, intellectual development varies tremendously from child to child. Even in eighth grade, only about one-third of the students can consistently demonstrate formal operations—that is, the ability to reason abstractly. Since many young adolescents are still at the concrete-operational stage of development, opportunities for experiential, hands-on learning are especially important to them. Giving young adolescents materials like mathematics manipulatives and hands-on science materials can facilitate their learning of important concepts and skills. It is also important for teachers to help young adolescents develop the "capacity to interpret symbols and deal with verbal ideas without having to manipulate physical objects" (National Middle School Association, 1982, p. 19). Thus, effective middle-level teachers pose challenging questions: "What if?" "What do you think will happen?" "Are you sure?" "How do you know?" "Why?"

Another way that teachers can attend to the wide variability among young adolescents is to identify the ways in which each student learns most effectively and to plan instruction accordingly. Yet the multiplicity of dimensions on which young adolescents differ makes tailoring instruction to their individual needs difficult at best. As Steven Levy, a former Massachusetts Teacher of the Year, told the Association of Experiential Education in October 1993: "When I think about meeting the needs of each child, I feel overwhelmed. Since these needs are virtually bottomless, I cannot hope to address them all." Instead, Levy tries to create an environment so rich that it brings out the "genius" in each child. He points out that, when we use the word *genius*, we usually think only of the most common definition: "extraordinary intellectual power." But this definition limits genius to a very few. By providing a rich classroom environment, Levy allows children to pursue their natural talents and inclinations, develop their own distinctive character, and build on their unique capacities and aptitudes—all equally valid, though less common, definitions of *genius*.

At the same time that young adolescents are learning to think more abstractly, they are searching for greater autonomy and independence. Thus, adapting curriculum and instruction to their needs also means helping them take responsibility for their own learning. By asking students to predict, draw conclusions, make inferences, and justify their answers, teachers can encourage students to move beyond the passive acquisition of information (National Middle School Association, 1982) to active learning. Good teachers foster students' independence by giving them opportunities to pose their own problems, choose their own topics of inquiry, and select their own reading materials.

To promote this kind of self-directed learning, teachers must change the traditional definition of their role. They must see themselves not as information-giver but as diagnostician, coach, resource person, facilitator, and evaluator. As Theodore Sizer put it in one of his nine principles of "essential" schools, "The governing metaphor of the school should be student as worker, rather than the more familiar metaphor of teacher as deliverer of instructional services" (1992, p. 208).

Early adolescence is also a time when friendship, social acceptance by peers, and a sense of belonging grow in importance. Thus cooperative learning methods are especially appropriate for middle school classrooms. "When students learn in small, carefully structured learning groups (with group goals, equal opportunity for success, and individual accountability) they help one another learn, gain in self-esteem and feelings of individual responsibility for their learning, and increase in respect and liking for their classmates" (George and Alexander, 1993, p. 160). Balancing such teams by race, gender, and academic ability also breaks down barriers among subgroups and fosters sensitivity to cultural diversity.

Still another characteristic of early adolescence is youngsters' growing interest in the larger world and increased capacity for empathy and role taking. It is not uncommon for young adolescents to become involved in heated discussions about justice and other ideals and to form their own opinions on important social issues. They are also struggling to make personal meaning out of their school experience. Personalizing curriculum and instruction means integrating themes that help students to see systems rather than disconnected facts (Carnegie Corporation, 1990, p. 13). These themes should be both socially significant and personally relevant (Beane, 1990).

Finally, personalizing curriculum and instruction means helping young adolescents find constructive ways to express their deep feelings. Effective middle-level teachers use art, poetry, music, drama, and other forms of creative expression to help their students share their thoughts, hopes, and fears with others.

Providing Comprehensive Support Services

Many educators feel that helping youngsters with their personal problems is not within the school's domain or the capacity of today's hard-pressed public school teacher. Yet it is impossible to meet many young adolescents' academic needs without addressing their social, emotional, and physical needs as well. This is especially true in poor, urban neighborhoods, where many children lack adequate nutrition and health care, and the problems associated with poverty, racism, and violence add to the normal developmental challenges of early adolescence.

Of vital importance, then, are comprehensive health services, including education, prevention, and treatment. As the Carnegie Corporation notes, "Good health does not guarantee that students will be interested in learning, but ample evidence suggests that poor health lowers students' academic performance" (1990, p. 20). Young adolescents need health education and preventive guidance to help protect themselves and others from unhealthy choices about smoking, eating, drugs, and sex. They also need access to appropriate mental health services—services that only 20 to 30 percent of those who need them now get. "Because of the link between health and school success, middle grade schools must ensure the accessibility of health and counseling services and function as health-promoting environments" (Carnegie Corporation, 1990, p. 20).

The Carnegie Corporation recommends that every school have a health coordinator to provide limited screening and treatment, make and monitor referrals to health services outside the school, and coordinate school health education and related activities. James Comer's School Development Program goes even further. It calls for a mental health team composed of all the health and mental health staff in the school, along with classroom teachers, to help establish schoolwide health policies, deal with overall health and climate issues, and tackle individual cases.

Middle school educators are quietly pioneering such efforts in Indiana and across the country. All the schools featured in this book have made a major commitment to providing comprehensive student assistance programs. They provide individual and group counseling, arrange for peer support groups, and design and implement classroom activities dealing with a range of health-related topics. In addition to working directly with youth, team members provide parent and teacher consultations; help identify individual differences, needs, and problems; and work with teachers, specialists, and administrators to develop schoolwide programs and solve specific problems. To serve those students whose needs exceed the school's in-house resources, they have developed links to health and mental health providers in local hospitals, community health centers, counseling centers, and youth-serving agencies.

School-based health clinics are another promising vehicle for providing comprehensive health services, especially because they make such services immediately accessible to students. Yet for a variety of reasons (not the least of which is cost) few middle schools have actually created such clinics. Harshman School in Indianapolis, which we describe in Chapter Three, is an outstanding exception. Its story provides a compelling example of the need for in-school health screening of young adolescents.

Linking Family, School, and Community

Generally, peers provide much needed support as young adolescents move from childhood to adulthood, from social conformity to personal autonomy. Yet the intense desire to fit in can have negative consequences for youngsters. Afraid of looking, sounding, or acting "different," they are often extremely self-conscious. They may be reluctant to pursue their own educational, cultural, or recreational interests if they deviate too far from those of their pals. The peer group can also exert powerful pressure to experiment with tobacco, alcohol, other drugs, sex, and other risky behaviors.

Parents and educators are sometimes tempted to back away during early adolescence, feeling powerless in the face of peer pressure. Nevertheless, most young adolescents still respect their parents' opinions and ideas, despite myths to the contrary (Sorenson, 1973). And they continue to look to their parents for affection, identification, values, and help in solving problems (Kandel and Lesser, 1972). As Ianni points out, "Adolescents do generate their own norms and rules, but this process does not and cannot develop in isolation from the institutional context of the communities in which they live and learn" (Ianni, 1989, p. 679).

Neither the home nor the school can afford to step aside. As Gayle Dorman writes, "Young people need adults to maintain the direction and momentum when they cannot. Above all, they need adults who care about them as they mature" (1987, p. 4). Personalizing middle schools means providing young adolescents with adult guidance and support. It also means aligning home and school, so that students receive a consistent message in both and are not attached to one at the expense of the other.

Dorman adds that during this period "children emerge from the world of here-and-now into a wider world of novel and panoramic possibilities. Their sense of personal achievement, competence, and commitment deepens; their understanding of life and of their future begins to take on new breadth and depth. They seek a new definition of themselves in the context of the larger world, and they bring great energy to their search" (1987, pp. 2–3).

As young adolescents struggle to discover themselves, they are beset by questions: Who am I? What does the future hold for me? What values are important to me? How can I make a difference in my community? Where do I fit in society at large? These questions are especially poignant for poor, urban youth who often have no clear vision of what is possible beyond high school or even middle school graduation.

Personalized middle schools help young adolescents undertake this search by extending learning beyond the school walls. They encourage community support for the school, while at the same time encouraging youth to explore their surrounding community and the world around them. Through career exploration programs, like the one created and managed by Mary Ley at Sarah Scott Middle School, they provide students with an expanded vision of the future.

Personalized middle schools also give young people an opportunity to build self-esteem and a sense of civic responsibility through community service. As Stevenson points out, "Young adolescents working together to do something that directly benefits others are able to see themselves in a new and developmentally valuable light" (1992, p. 130). Service projects promote social interaction with peers, younger children, older adolescents, and adult community members including each others' parents and grandparents. They provide opportunities for young adolescents to try out more adult roles and to learn firsthand about themselves, their peers, and those whom they serve. Through community service, students also discover the possibility that they can make a difference in the world around them. While the primary motivation for doing service is helping others, young adolescents often get more than they give—personal satisfaction, recognition, respect, and a deep appreciation for the value of serving others.

Responding to a Moral Imperative

The stories of the four middle schools in this book illustrate the great strides that are possible when educators share a vision of personalizing their educational program and are supported in that vision by critical friends and knowledgeable advisers. The administrators, teachers, counselors, nurses, and parents of these schools have all committed themselves to service—to serving poor, urban youth. Their stories give the lie to the gloomy predictions of those who say that our urban schools cannot change and should simply be abandoned.

Jonathan Kozol (1991) and other advocates play an important role in the fight to achieve better, more equitable public schools. By pointing out the dire plight of many of our urban schools, they generate outrage and garner public support for reform. Yet they often paint such negative portraits that the situation seems hopeless.

It is true that many urban young people are at risk from poor nutrition; inadequate health care; racism; unemployment; community disintegration; and the easy availability of drugs, alcohol, and guns. These conditions make schooling especially difficult. And the best efforts of educators are often hampered by deteriorating buildings, out-of-date materials and equipment, inadequate resources, and rigid bureaucracies.

Despite their many problems, however, urban youth are resilient, and so are their schools. The four schools you are about to meet teach us that the situation is serious but by no means hopeless. Their stories suggest that in poor, urban schools fundamental transformation is possible—and without large infusions of money. What it requires, at a minimum, is that we as a society respond to the moral imperative of caring for and educating *all* of our children. What it requires is a vision of effective middle schools and a belief that change is possible.

"How can teachers know the students," asks Theodore Sizer in *Horace's School*, "know them well enough to understand how their minds work, know where they come from, what pressures buffet them, what they are and are not disposed to do? A teacher cannot stimulate a child to learn without knowing that child's mind—the course of action necessary for an individual requires an understanding of the particulars" (1992, p. 40). Implicit in this statement is the added requirement that teachers know children's hearts as well as their minds and that they know the families and communities of which they are a part.

What can middle schools do to know their students well? How can they help each youngster grow and develop to his or her full potential? How can they attend to the particular needs of poor children in poor communities, coming from a staggering array of different racial, ethnic, and socioeconomic backgrounds? And how can school administrators, school systems, policy makers, governments, and private funding agencies effectively support the kind of fundamental change that is so urgently needed?

The answer, in our view, is in personalizing urban middle-level education. The answer is in developing a coherent, systemic, and yet highly individualized approach to the process of school change. The stories in the chapters that follow will, we hope, make the abstract concept of personalization come to life.

Chapter Two

Everybody Is Somebody

> Education is only a certain relationship which we
> establish between ourselves and our children, a
> certain climate in which feelings, instincts, and
> thoughts can flourish.
> —*Natalia Ginzburg*

It is a cliché of middle-grades reform efforts that schools should be more like families. In the small western Indiana city of Terre Haute we found a school that worked better than most families we know. Sarah Scott Middle School is a small school in the poorest section of the community. It succeeded, more than any other single school we visited, in making every student feel known and cared for.

The components of this success were extraordinarily complex and multifaceted. They included leadership of many kinds—among the school's administrators, teachers, and community members. Individuals and institutions outside the school, including the Lilly Endowment, also provided critical resources and support. And the catalyst that made the Sarah Scott brew so powerful seemed to be a pervasive spirit of openness and risk taking, best embodied in the person of one gentle, insightful man—Principal Carlos Aballi.

Aballi modeled, in his relationships with staff and students alike, the ethic of caring he was hoping to achieve. Sarah Scott illustrates how, with effective school-based leadership, a neighborhood school in a poor neighborhood can succeed.

A Neighborhood School in a Poor Neighborhood

Terre Haute lies on the Wabash River at the western edge of Indiana near the Illinois line, seventy-three miles west-southwest of Indianapolis. Once one of the chief manufacturing centers in the

Midwest, it has experienced a major decline in both its manufacturing base and its population, which now numbers just over a hundred thousand.

Approximately seventeen thousand students attend schools in the Vigo County system, which includes Terre Haute. At the time of our visits, fewer than five hundred youngsters—grades seven through nine—were enrolled at Sarah Scott, making it the smallest of the county's six junior high schools. (After our visits, Sarah Scott and the five other junior high schools in the county moved to a sixth- through eighth-grade configuration, and its name changed from Sarah Scott Junior High School to Sarah Scott Middle School.)

Sarah Scott is a neighborhood school. The neighborhood is mainly working-class and poor. Many parents are unemployed. There are two public housing projects in Terre Haute, and Sarah Scott serves them both. School counselors estimate that half the students live in single-parent homes. Twelve to 15 percent of the students are classified as learning disabled or mentally or emotionally handicapped. Blacks make up 15 percent of the student body—the highest percentage in the city.

The staff at Sarah Scott deals every day with the effects of poverty, neglect, family violence, and abuse. "These young people are the most incredible survivors that you'd ever want to lay your eyes on," Judy Elsey, a science teacher, told us. "They're incredible people, because they are victims in their own homes."

"The kids have real problems," said Tom Taylor, who teaches social studies and heads the eighth-grade team. "Our team meets twice a week. We need more meeting time. The first thing on our agenda is the students' problems and concerns. Then, later, we deal with the principal's agenda and all the paperwork. First thing, kids. We call them in to congratulate them. We call them in to chew them out. We call them in to hug them.

"One kid's brother just murdered a guy," Taylor went on. "He's having problems. One kid's father is about to be executed for murder. This poor kid—he's got it all up against him. We call him in and talk with him."

Lana Shuck, who taught classes in parenting and child development to ninth graders at Sarah Scott before the transition, told us of being devastated when she first learned she was being transferred from her job at a local high school to Sarah Scott. "I came here from South High with tears in my eyes," she said. "I thought it was the worst thing that could ever happen to me. Instead, it was the best thing that ever happened to me."

"Lana is the best example we have," said computer science teacher Steve Lingenfelter, "of what this school can do to you if you let it—what the kids can do. You get so much satisfaction working here, because you know you're the only salvation some of these kids have got. You're it. They go home to nothing. Drunk parents—if they're there. Beatings, and sexual abuse. We know."

"Many of our students virtually raise themselves," said Assistant Principal Sandra Kelley. "There is no adult, maybe from Monday to Friday. The only meals they eat, often, are here at school."

"Everybody Is Somebody"

Helping students from an impoverished community envision a positive future and find meaning in their school lives is the challenge of working at Sarah Scott Middle School. "With a lot of kids," Principal Aballi told us, "when you ask them to think about the future and you say, 'What do you see?' they say, 'I don't see nothing.' We want our kids to see something. We want them to start thinking about their possible selves. To start dreaming a little bit. And our staff are more and more taking risks to try new teaching strategies to address the unique needs of kids, to move beyond the school to make connections with the outside world, to provide learning opportunities for kids who don't otherwise have the means."

We found ample evidence during our visits to Sarah Scott of the kind of risk taking Aballi was talking about among students and teachers alike. They were not just willing but eager to develop innovative programs, to talk about controversial issues, to admit to personal and policy failures, to work in teams with people of contrary viewpoints, to be willing to change themselves. And they took these risks in an overall context of severely limited resources, general indifference from the central school administration, and, sometimes, disdain or outright hostility from the larger community.

While Sarah Scott still had its problems at the time of our visits, the staff had succeeded in making students feel known, respected, and valued. "It's like our school motto," said one student. "Everybody is somebody here. All the teachers know you by name."

Administrators and teachers alike are also quite willing to give out hugs when necessary. Assistant Principal Kelley told us that young adolescents, and even high school students, need physical affection. "You know, with secondary students, you're always told you must not touch them," she said. "Hogwash. We do it all the time here, and I think that's what a lot of our kids need. They need that parenting—the touching that goes along with parenting. So we do it. I even have hug coupons. I keep them on my desk and every once in a while a kid has a problem, comes in, and I give him a coupon. It says, 'Free—One hug, whenever you need it.'"

Mary Ann Sparks is the mother and stepmother of three girls, Kelly, Corinna, and Christina, who attended Sarah Scott. Kelly, the eldest, described the Sarah Scott she knew ten years earlier in four words: "It was a hole." Today's Sarah Scott is a very different school.

When we asked Mrs. Sparks what makes the new Sarah Scott work, she had a hard time answering. "I really don't know," she said. "The teachers here seem to really care. I think the kids relate to Mr. Aballi. He's willing to get out there on the basketball floor with them once in a while or joke with them. The kids seem to have a voice here. Mr. Aballi is positive. He tells them, 'You are somebody.'"

"*You are somebody,*" she said again, almost in a whisper. "Other principals don't say that kind of thing. The leadership needs to be positive. How can the kids believe in themselves if the leaders don't?"

A School Transformed

"The bottom line is getting our kids to feel good about themselves as learners," Aballi began when we sat down with him in his office on our first visit to Sarah Scott. "We are moving in that direction. We have made a lot of changes. Sometimes it appears that we take two or three steps forward, and other times it looks as though we're going back. I attribute that to the process of change."

Aballi paused. The walls of his office were adorned with plaques, citations, banners, diplomas, framed quotations about children and schooling (such as "The Seven Needs of Young Adolescents"), charts, pictures, a prayer, and other memorabilia. He pointed at some snapshots of fifteen beaming students on the wall behind us. "That is my advisory, by the way," he said, referring to the small group of youngsters he met with three times a week. "Those are my kids."

Those first few moments with Aballi contain many of the essential elements of the educational and human values that drive both this man and his school. His philosophy starts and ends with the kids—their needs as learners and as young adolescents, and their hunger for close relationships with adults who will take ownership of the huge responsibility of nurturing their minds and spirits. "Those are my kids."

In between is the slow, painful process of change and his recognition of its frustrations. Aballi and the staff at Sarah Scott were remarkably willing to discuss their failures and admit their flaws. There is a connection, no doubt, between this kind of candor and a person's (or a school's) openness to change.

Sarah Scott has made enormous changes since Aballi became principal in 1986 (one year before MGIP came to Terre Haute), both in school climate and student outcomes. While the proportion of its students qualifying for free or reduced-price lunches rose from 46.5 percent in 1987 to 61.9 percent in 1992 (paralleling the trend in local plant closings and unemployment), Sarah Scott's average daily attendance rate steadily increased, test scores held steady in math while rising significantly in reading (in both areas, the scores were well above anticipated achievement levels for both white and minority students), expulsions and suspensions were reduced (though the number of suspensions remained relatively high), and corporal punishment was abolished.

Even more important, perhaps, was the less easily quantified change in atmosphere. For years, Sarah Scott had been known as the roughest of Terre Haute's six junior high schools, home of the city's largest group of "problem" (meaning poor and black) kids.

"When I was growing up in the seventies," said one Sarah Scott teacher who is a Terre Haute native, "Sarah Scott was *the* inner-city school. I went to Otter Creek Junior High, on the north side. There were a lot of racial problems at Sarah Scott. When we would run track or play football against them, there was usually a police escort. It got a real bad name."

"For years before Carlos arrived," said one district administrator, "Sarah Scott had been a very formalized institution, where rules and regulations were the guide. You broke this rule, you were out. If you can learn this way, fine. If not, quit."

"This was the worst school in the county," said art teacher Mary Ley, another Terre Haute native. "If you said you taught at Sarah Scott, people would say you're crazy or laugh at you."

Aballi himself was reluctant to speak in such stark terms or criticize Sarah Scott's previous administrations. Instead, he took pains to point out the school's long history and the fact that dedicated teachers and good programs were there before his own arrival. Indeed, Sarah Scott's reputation in the community as a "rough school" was almost certainly an exaggeration—a reflection of racial and social-class stereotyping—even in the old days. When pressed, though, Aballi acknowledged that the school's old program was not appropriate for young adolescents. "They put a lot of effort into controlling the kids based on fear in the old days," he said. "I say, dare to get gentle with kids, and you come out ahead."

Aballi's "dare to get gentle" approach produced dramatic results. Vandalism and graffiti disappeared, and at the time of our visits the seventy-five-year-old school building on South Ninth Street was neat, clean, and inviting, even if the fixtures were outdated and the roof leaked here and there. The corridors were lined with paintings, posters, and displays of students' work. Violent confrontations and racial tension had been greatly reduced. The school seemed to overflow with a sense of mutual respect, responsibility, affection, and even tenderness between students and staff. Again and again, students told us that the best thing about the school was the teachers: "They really care about us." "The teachers respect you." "It's like a family."

"I see at Sarah Scott the most dramatic turnaround of a staff in any of our schools," said Assistant Superintendent RamonaWedding, "or in any junior high school I have visited across the country."

An Eighth Grader's View: "You Feel Like You Belong"

Billy Bones is one of Carlos's kids. When he started seventh grade at Sarah Scott, he was assigned to the principal's adviser-advisee program. He was not inclined to like school and had a record as a troublemaker.

"Billy has changed a lot," said Aballi. "He used to tend to be negative and very sarcastic. Now he's become more positive and feels better about himself."

We met Billy toward the end of his eighth-grade year and asked him what he thought of Sarah Scott. "It's a good school because the teachers really get along with the students," he said. "If you have problems with something, they'll give up their time and help you on it. I really like our principal and all the other office people. When you need help, you go to them. It's kind of small, so you know everybody here and you feel like it's a family. You feel like you belong."

Like other students we interviewed, Billy cited the quality of instruction as one of the school's strong points. "I really like my classes because a lot of them are hands-on," he said. "In science we made our own weather equipment and we're doing our own forecasts. The teachers try not to use the book because they think the book is boring."

Early in Billy's eighth-grade year Aballi chose him to be one of ten Sarah Scott representatives on the Leadership Task Force of Terre Haute, a citywide program for middle school students that is a partnership between Indiana State University and other community organizations. Aballi picked Billy, he said, because "we wanted to select kids who normally would not participate in this kind of activity. Billy is the type of kid who has the desire to lead, to get involved, but has no real means to do that."

The students in the task force work with adult mentors from the community; Billy's was Max Miller of the Purdue University Extension Agency. Miller and Billy regularly went places together both to learn and to have fun—from visiting a maple syrup–making operation, to going to a science fair, to attending local school board meetings to see how decisions about education are made. The students in the task force have a citywide meeting once a month; in addition, the Sarah Scott members meet twice a month with leaders, or "guides," from the university to take part in role-playing and other leadership exercises.

"At our last meeting," Billy explained, "we had one kid leave the room and our guide said, 'That person's a new kid in school.' Then that kid came back in, and we acted like we would to a new kid. We did the same thing with the person being a bully, a nerd—things like that.

"The person doesn't know what he is when he walks in the room. We start treating him like that, and then he figures out what he is and tells us how he felt about the way we treated him. Then we'll know how to fix it and how to treat people like that in real life—normal, like everybody else."

We asked Billy whether the experience had actually changed his attitudes toward other students. "Oh, yeah," he said earnestly. "Everybody in a group always classifies people. But now we try to minimize our classifying. We try to treat everybody normal. Like, if we have an after-school function, we actually invite people we'd never even dream of inviting before. People that nobody really talks to.

"This was something we did on our own—skills we learned at the program that we took into our own life. We talked about it after class. Some of us decided to do it. There was a party going on that weekend, so we invited a couple of them."

"What happened after the party?" we asked. "Did those kids become more friendly?"

"Yeah," Billy said with a laugh. "Very. Now they actually talk. Some of them we never even knew could talk. We actually hear them now. Now every time there's something like that we all try to invite one or two people."

"Does that make you feel different about yourself?" we asked.

"It makes me feel that I'm trying to help somebody who's not one of the more popular kids in school to make more friends," said Billy. "It's something I really like to do."

"Do you feel you have more of a special place in the school because you're on the Leadership Task Force?" we asked.

"Well," said Billy after thinking it over, "everybody's special here."

The Need to Be Known

What were the essential elements of change at Sarah Scott? How was it able to make the transition from a formalized, rule-driven institution to a humanistic, inclusive school? Even though it had not yet changed to its current middle school structure of sixth through eighth grade (which happened a year and a half after our visits), it functioned more as a true middle school than as a traditional junior high.

Its small size was certainly one factor. Many educators now recognize that the traditional large secondary school creates an atmosphere of anonymity that is antithetical to learning and growth—particularly in communities at risk. The Central Park East Secondary School in New York's East Harlem, which has achieved remarkable successes working with inner-city students, is organized around the "core conviction that all students—particularly poor students—need a school small enough to instill the sense that someone cares about them and holds them accountable," wrote Susan Chira in a *New York Times* profile of Deborah Meier, the school's founder and principal.

"Most human beings need to be known," Meier told the *Times*, "and it is more critical when other things are also fragile. Kids are dying in these large schools." Central Park East serves about five hundred students, virtually the same number as Sarah Scott. Aballi's school included only the seventh through ninth grades, however, while Meier's encompasses seventh through twelfth.

Another similarity between the two schools was their advisory programs, in which each full-time faculty member was responsible for getting to know a group of fifteen students well, meeting with them regularly, and serving as a counselor and mentor. At Sarah Scott, this included the principal.

"We want to get as many adults as possible involved," said Aballi, "so that we can keep the student-teacher ratio down. I like to be involved. It gives me an opportunity to get close to fifteen or so students. Also, our staff is basically secondary trained, like myself." (He came to Sarah Scott from an assistant principal's job at a high school.) "This way, they can see that I am also making an effort to make this program work for our kids."

Sarah Scott's advisory system was in its third year of operation when we visited. "To be honest with you," said Aballi, "it works very well with some teachers and doesn't work very well with others. We had a little money from the first MGIP grant that we used to train teachers, but we had to do it rather rapidly. It was just half a day of training—a brief introduction. We really need to follow up and give teachers opportunities to talk and share and see what has worked and what hasn't."

The lack of sufficient staff development and follow-up training for the advisory program was only one problem. The school schedule, hamstrung by budget constraints and the divergent state-mandated curricular and class-time requirements of the ninth grade, could not accommodate more than three twenty-minute advisory periods and two short team planning meetings per week. It simply was not enough time for many teachers, not used to coping with the extraordinary personal demands of the teacher-student advisory model.

"We hope that with the change to the middle school plan and adopting more middle school concepts we will be able to offer every teacher a common planning period *and* an individual planning period," said Aballi. "But we are operating under very difficult budgetary times. I don't know if that's going to be possible. We're going to have to use some creativity to provide for that."

Sarah Scott is not the only MGIP school that has had trouble establishing a fully successful advisory system. Many middle school teachers, trained to work in high schools, strongly resist the idea that they must be counselors as well as instructors. Indeed, the Vigo County Teachers Association considers the addition of advisory periods and team-based guidance (TBG) time to classroom teachers' duties to be contract issues. The teachers' union actually blocked these changes at some of the other Vigo County junior high schools.

"We have a long way to go—I mean, countywide," said Aballi. "And that makes it difficult for us here. Middle school is hard work. You cannot just get the kids busy and then go home at three o'clock. And teachers talk among themselves. They see our teachers doing advisory and TBG, and they talk. Those could very well be considered additional preparations and they could file a grievance. In other schools they're fighting advisory; they did away with advisory because of that."

Aballi recognized that he could not take a strong stance with his teachers. He could not say, "Look, you really need to improve your skills and work with your kids. What can I do to help you out?" He knew that they could reply, "Hey, look, I don't have to do this." Afraid that pushing too hard with the advisory program might jeopardize other programs already in place, he was reluctant to take that kind of risk. Instead, he took a different sort of risk: he led by example.

Mr. Aballi's Open Door

"We did all kinds of things in Mr. Aballi's advisory last year," eighth grader David Born told us. "He had parties for us—doughnuts, pizza. He talked to us a lot and encouraged us to do better in grades and helped us along.

"I don't think I would have been doing very well if it wasn't for him. I was really kind of bad last year—a terrible student. I had a bad attitude—macho.

"He would talk to me. He makes time for you. Even if he has a lot of work, his office is always open. The door is never shut, so you can go in there and talk to him whenever you want to. It makes you feel kind of good. In some of my other schools, the door was always closed. You didn't have nobody to talk to.

"Mr. Burton, the counselor, is good about that, too. You could go down there and talk to him about your problems without having to worry about them being all around the school. Mr. Aballi and Mr. Burton are really trustworthy. Whatever you say to them, it's just between you and them.

"Me and Mr. Aballi would have little talks and it helped me want to do better. Last year I got Bs, Cs, and Ds. This year, As, Bs, some Cs. It's better to have good grades."

David was excited about his upcoming field trip to Chattanooga with Mr. Taylor, his history teacher. "He's a leader," said David. "He's the kind of guy that will make things go. It's fun to be in his history class because he makes you feel like you were there. You'll think you were fighting in the Civil War. He makes it come alive. The Chattanooga trip was all his idea. We're going to walk the battlefield exactly as they did. We're going to hide behind the hill and charge at them like they did in the Civil War.

"It's gonna be fun. I'm not sure if Mr. Aballi will go. That'd be good. He gets involved with fun stuff. He's not the kind of principal that sits behind a desk, puts his feet up, and does paperwork. He comes out and does things with us. He wouldn't make you do anything that he wouldn't do himself. We went on a camp-out at the beginning of the year, and he came with us and stayed the night. Everything that we did, he did.

"He makes time on his own time. He doesn't just come to school and do this because he's being paid. He enjoys it. He comes to basketball games and mixers. He'll volunteer. He and Mr. Taylor have helped kids with their fundraisers. He'll come on his own weekend time to sit out there with them, because they have to have a guardian with them. He doesn't have to do that."

The powerful effects on boys like David of having a close relationship with a mentor like Aballi are obvious. "I just want to do good now," David said. "Mr. Aballi encouraged me to get good grades so I can go on to college and be somebody when I grow up. He is somebody. Even though he came from Cuba, which might be known as a bad country, he changed his life.

"I imagine that he was probably like me when he was a little kid," David told us. "I want to go to college and get a good job, have a nice family and a nice house. You don't have to live in a big mansion. I just want to be able to enjoy my job. I don't want to do something I hate.

"I want to be like Mr. Aballi. He enjoys his job. I look up to him. A lot of kids do."

"A Perfect Match"

If, as Judy Elsey said, many of the students at Sarah Scott are survivors, they may feel more at home in Carlos Aballi's school because he, too, is a kind of survivor. He is a soft-spoken, gentle, unprepossessing man in a job that traditionally called for a no-nonsense disciplinarian with a megaphone voice. His swarthy complexion and the mildly lilting remnants of his Cuban accent inevitably mark him as an outsider in an inbred and provincial school system. He does not readily volunteer details of his own personal struggle or the roadblocks he has faced in his work, but clearly they have affected him.

"I was born in Cuba and came to the United States on January 1, 1961, two years after Castro," Aballi told us. "We lived in Florida. My parents had been attorneys in Cuba, but with little English they had few options. They had some money saved, so they decided to invest in a business, and they bought a lunch truck. We worked at that for three years. Then there was a program sponsored by the Ford Foundation to train professionals to become teachers in Indiana. Both of my parents applied, and they were accepted.

"I know this sounds funny, but we came to Indiana like frontier people. We really didn't know what Indiana was like. The snow was very frightful. But we made it. My parents had to take education courses, and they had to take English, and they had to student teach. They became teachers.

"That's what brought us to Terre Haute. It's a good place to live. I'm very involved in our community, and I believe in that. One of the things we have done here is open up the community so that our kids feel they are part of it. And we have opened up the doors, too, for community people to come in, to have some input in the education of the children. It's a risk, and at first perhaps not totally accepted by the faculty, but it is more and more accepted."

Did Aballi experience special problems in his career because of his Cuban origins? Racial prejudice in Indiana can be subtle. One district administrator, who generally spoke well of Aballi, said, "When you see him for the first time, you think, boy, did somebody blow it. This is not a principal. This is not an administrator. This is not a leader. This is just a guy out here who's working with kids. Then, as you sit back and watch him, it's amazing. Of course, he wouldn't fit well everywhere, but it's a perfect match there. What he's been able to do for those kids is just tremendous."

The difference between this administrator and Aballi is the difference between "those kids" and "our kids."

The Education of a Middle School Principal

Like much of his staff, Aballi was trained to work in high schools. When he learned that he was to become principal at Sarah Scott, he set out to educate himself about middle schools and the needs of young adolescents. "I started reading," he said. "I read Joan Lipsitz's books, attended conferences and meetings. I visited schools that had exemplary programs, like in Louisville. I heard about the Noe Middle School there, which Joan wrote about in her book, *Successful Schools for Young Adolescents,* and I visited other Louisville schools, like Lassiter and Thomas Jefferson. What I learned there had a very positive effect on the way I do things today. The reorganization of our school structure—the movement to middle school from junior high school—makes this an exciting time. I like being part of that."

Aballi's move to Sarah Scott coincided with the Lilly Endowment's MGIP initiative in Vigo County, which proved to have a profound effect on his professional development. He took advantage of every opportunity to be exposed to new ideas. Responding to an invitation to Indiana school administrators from the endowment, he became a Lilly Fellow, which enabled him to attend numerous professional meetings and conferences. In addition, Aballi attended the Principals Institute at the Harvard Graduate

School of Education for two weeks in the summer, again with the help of Lilly funds.

One of the endowment's recommendations was that schools begin with a detailed self-assessment guided by the Middle Grades Assessment Program (MGAP) created by Gayle Dorman and others at the Center for Early Adolescence at the University of North Carolina. MGAP is designed to enable a school-based assessment team of staff and parents to develop a comprehensive measure of the school's responsiveness to the needs of young adolescents and to produce a plan for improving the school.

Only two of the six Vigo County junior highs completed the MGAP process initially. Five years after the Middle Grades Improvement Program came to Terre Haute, the other junior highs and their principals were still struggling with the notion of self-assessment. But Aballi's openness to learning and change in his own professional life, coupled with the opportunities made available through the endowment, enabled him to internalize quickly the principles underlying the middle school reform movement. He became an early champion of the value of MGAP, and he believes that the self-assessment process had a great impact on his staff.

"MGAP was what we used to begin," he said. "It was really a qualitative assessment—assessing the quality of the relationship between the teacher and the student, between the school and the home. Those are really the important things—not looking at how many chairs there are in the library and how many books. It got us off to a good start, and it was good staff development as well."

As science teacher Elsey commented, "The MGAP set us up for the changes to come."

Asserting and Sharing Authority

Aballi seemed to know instinctively when to push and when to back off, when to rely on group decision making and when to assert his own authority. No one at Sarah Scott described him as author-itarian, and yet the move to middle school principles and the MGAP process were two instances when he made no accommo-dation for footdraggers.

"I told the teachers," Aballi said, "we're going into the Middle Grades Improvement Program. Everybody participates, and every-body will have an opportunity to benefit."

At other times, he could be just as insistent that others take responsibility for researching issues and making decisions. As James Comer recommends in his carefully developed, process-oriented approach to school change, Aballi encouraged groups to come to consensus rather than voting on an issue. He instinctively recog-nized that when people vote, there are winners and losers. When they come to consensus, everybody wins.

"We have an MGIP Advisory Committee that is involved in how we spend the Lilly money here at school," said Aballi. "At the first meeting, one member said, 'You make the decision. That's what you get paid to do.' When I wouldn't, she came back and said, 'Well, just divide the money equally.' And I said no. I want to look at what our overall needs are and then *as a group* decide what is best for our school.

"I had everybody write out lists of needs, compiled them, and passed them out. They had a chance to look at them, then we came together. This is the amount of money we have. These are the needs. Everybody had a chance to talk.

"We started voting and I said, 'Nope. We're not going to vote. We need to agree, even if it takes a little bit longer.' It worked really well, because we do have a good faculty. They respect one another, as people and as professionals.

"It took a bit longer, but it was worth it. That same person who said, 'You make the decision,' came back to me the next day and said, 'You know, you were right. It really didn't take that much longer to do what you wanted, and we feel good about what we have done.'"

"Carlos has a unique way," said Assistant Superintendent Wedding, "of empowering teachers and letting them be in charge enough to try whatever they want to try, and yet he has that safety net there, so that if it doesn't work it's okay. 'I'm here to catch you. It will be all right.' That's the way he works. It creates teachers who are always looking for something different to do that will help their kids learn better. It creates teachers who are willing to examine any possibility."

Curricular Priorities:
"What Do We Want These Kids to Know?"

Judy Elsey's ninth-grade life science class was buzzing with purposeful activity. The students were working in groups of three or four, conducting a "discovery lab." They were dropping liquids into petri dishes, preparing slides, studying them under microscopes, writing up their results. When we first came into the room, it was hard to find the teacher. Students were standing up, talking in groups, moving around the room to different work stations—and many of these ninth graders were considerably larger than Elsey, who was at last discovered working with a student who was having a hard time getting his microscope image in focus.

"Right today we have daphnia," Elsey explained, "which are small crustacea, in the scopes. I give them a problem: What is the effect of alcohol—in this case, gin—on daphnia? And so we've had them go into morbid spasms this morning. We've had them die instantly. This is what happens once you get this percentage of alcohol in a living system.

"We start with a concept, and then we take it wherever it goes. Sometimes they find the concept. And then we say, OK, what did we see? What happened here? It's discovery-based science. We don't do a lot of cookbook, recipe-type experimentation. I figure we'll leave that to the professionals. Let's not remake the wheel six or seven times. Let's turn the kids loose and let them find the wheel."

Elsey, who was named the Indiana Biology Teacher of the Year for 1991–92, started teaching at Sarah Scott years before Carlos Aballi came on the scene. But just about the time of his arrival she underwent a personal transformation that mirrored the changes he would bring about as principal.

"I was trying to think whether I'd get out of this business or stay in it," she said. "I seriously looked at getting out. Then I went to a convention in Chicago. I was sitting, listening to some guy talk about the phylogenic approach to biology. And I'm thinking, what does this have to do with my kids? Eighty percent of them are never going to have another life science course. I have one shot at them. It was one of those things where you say, 'Wow. Where are we?'

"I got back from that convention, I went down to the assistant superintendent's office, and I said I wanted to throw out the whole ninth-grade curriculum. He said, 'You're kidding.' I said no. I want to base it on issues. I want to have a scientifically literate citizenry. I want them to see the tie-in between life outside this room and life inside this room.

"He said, 'OK, Judy. Go do it. But you have to tie in 75 or 80 percent of the regular biology curriculum.' I said, not only will I take that in, but I want to take in earth science, some chemistry, and physics, because you can't teach those things without getting into those other disciplines. And I did it.

"The second thing I did was go to a workshop by the National Science Foundation on genetics. We had morning classes from 8:00 to 12:30. I thought I would die. I thought, this is what my kids are doing. They're sitting in a classroom. I'm a 'sage on the stage,' and they're taking notes. No wonder they're yawning. These are fourteen-year-olds that have more hormones going than Carter's got little liver pills."

So Elsey came home and took a hard look at the curriculum. She asked some tough questions: "What are my priorities? What do I really want these kids to know?" Then, she decided to "throw out all that stuff" and start all over again.

"We're into the issues," she told us. During one class, students debated the pros and cons of screening the population for the HIV virus. In another session, Elsey brought up the subject of a young man with AIDS who had passed HIV along to two hundred young boys. Then, she asked the students to talk about it. Her goal is to get her students to learn to think.

Elsey described her approach this way: "I say, 'What do you think?' At first they look at me and they say, 'I don't think anything.' And I say, 'Wait a minute. You cannot sit in my classroom and not have some opinion. I'm not asking you to name the cell structure.' Now they're getting to the point where they say, 'Yeah, I've got an opinion.'

"When we do genetics, I start out by having them cut out snowflakes. We put them all around the room, and they have to put their names on the front of them. They are all different, and they are all precious, and they are all good. They are genetically unique. That's okay. That's the way it's supposed to be. Nature tends toward variation, not toward the norm.

"We do a lot with genetics. I don't get to the abortion issue other than taking twenty genetic disorders that they're familiar with. I make them write them down in a list, and then they have to draw the line where they'd abort a pregnancy. Some will not abort any— not even little Baby Teresa who was born without a brain. I tell them, 'I don't care where the line comes.' They get fifteen points for doing it. I just want them to think. They tell me that's my hardest assignment. They'll sit here and agonize and agonize."

Summing it all up, Elsey said, "You learn to respect each other, and you learn there are no right answers. Life doesn't have a whole lot of right answers. And that's as valuable as anything I can teach."

The Relationship Between Active Learning
and Classroom Discipline

Another aspect of her former teaching style that dissatisfied Elsey was her approach to maintaining classroom discipline: "I didn't have many problems in my classroom, but once I disciplined somebody we weren't friends anymore." She discovered that changing her teaching methods by incorporating more active, hands-on experiences for the students had an immediate effect on her relations with them.

"Once you have something they're interested in," she explained, "they're working like beavers. And you're free and loose to go around the room. You're twice as busy, you walk twice as much and work twice as hard, but you're there and you can say, 'How are you doing today?' You can touch, you can lay that hand on and say, 'How was Mom last night? Did it go OK at home?' And so you get rid of the problems that were being created from your not being able to touch base with them on a one-to-one basis.

"I love Sarah Scott," Elsey added, "because it's been the crucible, the place where I have had the freedom to develop who I am and what I want. The philosophy here is 'Why not?' We wanted to put together a group with Otter Creek Junior High on genetic justice. I told Carlos what I wanted to do and he said, 'Go do it.' So we got ourselves five lawyers and debated a surrogate mother case right in the federal courthouse downtown."

The sheer excitement and stimulation of working in such an open environment, in which freedom and experimentation are core values, is surely part of what held the Sarah Scott faculty together. "I don't know why this faculty works together as well as it does," Elsey reflected, "because you couldn't ask for a bigger group of different personalities. We can yell at each other and even have violent disagreements, and then we're back working. I don't know how to explain it."

Later, talking about the staff's commitment to the welfare of the students, she hit upon a possible answer. "When you go down the hall," she said, "and look at how people feel about these kids—they really care. From the students' point of view, that's their strength. They'll go the extra mile. They're ready to listen to their problems." Ever the scientist, she tested this theory in her mind. "Some are going to slam their doors at 3:20 and go home," she admitted. "I expect you have that in every building. But there are a lot of folks still here late in the day. And there's a lot of folks that kids come and cry to.

"That's our ultimate strength. That's probably the cement that keeps us together, when it comes right down to it: What is going to be best for these kids?"

The Firing of Mrs. Ditto

A turning point in the transformation of Sarah Scott occurred in the second year after Carlos Aballi became principal. He faced the necessity of removing a teacher whom he considered incompetent and, despite his efforts to help her change, ultimately intransigent.

"When I came here," Aballi explained, "we had a veteran staff. I wanted to really pursue middle school concepts. I wanted us to be more child oriented. I wanted to take some chances.

"We had an eighth-grade teacher here who was very damaging. This was 'Mrs. Ditto.' She gave the kids a lot of busywork. She did a lot of things that really led to nothing. We had kids coming to the counselor and saying, 'We are not learning anything. We're not going to be prepared for the ninth grade.'

Aballi worked with her for a year, developing an improvement plan that outlined the things she needed to do. Not much changed, however. So, Aballi worked with her for a second year. At the same time he got the local teachers' association involved. Together, they developed another improvement plan, very similar to the first. It, too, was unsuccessful.

"She fought me to the end," said Aballi. "She became defiant. We decided to meet every two weeks. She taped all of our conversations. It was not pleasant." Finally, in the spring of the second year, having tried his best, Aballi recommended that Mrs. Ditto be let go.

We asked Aballi why he did not try to have her transferred to another school. "Well," he said, "I thought about that. Then I thought, how would I feel if a person like that came to my school? I didn't want to do that to anyone else." So, Aballi took a stand— and he won.

"To make a long story short," he said, "we went into a full-blown hearing before the school board, lasting a couple of months. About thirty people testified. I was questioned for four hours straight regarding the whole procedure. When it came time for her side to present their case and call their witnesses, they decided not to call anyone. They gambled that, based on what had been presented, the school board would not go forward with it. But the board voted to let her go.

"That was three years ago. At that time, I really didn't know how this staff would react, because she had been here a lot longer than I had. But it was fantastic. I think they saw how I operated and that I tried to be fair."

Other school officials confirmed that the dismissal of Mrs. Ditto had a profound effect on Sarah Scott. It helped establish Aballi's credibility as a tough administrator. "He let them know that he was going to stick it out," said Ramona Wedding, "and he wasn't going to tolerate less than what was best for the kids. He did a terrific job of taking all the right legal steps and the documentation. It had needed to be done for many years."

Judy Johnston, former director of the Schenley High School Teacher Center in Pittsburgh and an MGIP consultant to Vigo County, pointed out that Aballi was required by law to follow the lengthy process of working with Mrs. Ditto, giving her a chance to improve her performance. But Johnston also noted that few principals in Vigo County, or other school districts for that matter, have had the stomach to remove incompetent teachers. "His handling of that case signaled the staff that he was the educational leader in that school," she said. "And what is really significant is that he did it in a school system that had not sent any clear signals to teachers about how they should teach."

Mary Ley's Truth

One significant side effect of Aballi's dogged efforts to dismiss Mrs. Ditto was that other marginal or burned-out teachers at Sarah Scott saw the writing on the wall and decided to leave on their own. By 1992, Aballi's sixth year as principal, about two-thirds of the staff were people he had hired.

One of the first of these was art teacher Mary Ley, who also teaches Quest, a course in skills for adolescence, and runs the school's career awareness program. Ley came to Sarah Scott after teaching at another Terre Haute junior high. "I felt good with the kids there," she said, "but never felt good with that staff. There was a real hard-core teacher there who was always griping about kids in the teachers' lunchroom. He was always saying, 'This kid's going to be a slut.' And I really got tired of hearing it.

"About the fourth time I heard it, I said, 'You know, you really make me sick. You're burnt out. You should get out of this. Because I wasn't a perfect kid in junior high either, and I turned out fine. You can't judge a kid at the junior high level.' Everybody stood up and applauded. But those same teachers had sat there for years and listened to this guy!"

Aballi, for his part, attributes a significant part of the change at Sarah Scott to Ley. "When we first started introducing middle school ideas," he said, "we had a mostly veteran staff that was trained to work in secondary schools. You've read stories about teachers' lounges where everybody goes to complain and put the kids down? That was our lounge! But Mary would get up and speak her truth. And she always did it in such a beautiful way that people would applaud, or sometimes they wouldn't be able to say anything."

Ley was one of many teachers at Sarah Scott who felt that the school lacked sorely needed resources and was not getting its fair share compared with schools in wealthier neighborhoods. "Our students here, who come from the projects, or the group homes, kids who are struggling—they have *real* needs and problems," she said. "We don't even have a conference area in this school for kids. I'd have my career awareness program going Monday through Friday if I could, but we don't have an auditorium. I literally have to kick the choir teacher out of the music room on Tuesdays and Thursdays to run my program.

"I run every day," Ley continued. "Some days I run purposely through the streets that the kids live on. So I really understand why some days maybe they're a little bit hungry, maybe they're a little bit cold, angry, bitter. When I see what they're living in, I can perceive why they're acting the way they do. Kids are smarter than we're giving them credit for. They may not be smart mathematically or in grammar, but they are very smart in the way they perceive the falsehoods that we sometimes give them."

Like many public school teachers, Ley often feels frustrated and angry about her job. "I have real downs," she said. "I get angry, but I don't take it out on kids." Instead, she takes it out on the pavement. "I could not make it a day without a seven- to ten-mile run," said Ley. "Saturdays it's fifteen. Sundays it's twelve.

"A two-mile run wouldn't do it for me. The first mile's usually an ugly mile. I'm angry. I'm angry at a kid that might have told another teacher to 'fuck off.' I'm angry that a kid would say that. I've never had a kid say that to me. But even the most perfect teacher with the most perfect little bow blouses and the most perfect little feet in the most perfect little pumps and the most perfect little hair and little beads who doesn't understand the kids but only understands her subject—even *she* does not deserve to be told that.

"So the first mile is ugly. The second mile is a little less ugly, the third mile less. By the time I get to six and seven, I see things— like a squirrel climbing a tree, or a hawk in the sky. It puts life in perspective.

"I think colleges are teaching teachers wrong. They teach them how to teach their subjects, but until we understand kids and understand why they hurt inside, they aren't even going to listen to us. One of the worst feelings kids have—and adults, too—is rejection. They've all experienced some kind of rejection. I've been working with one girl for three years to feel good about herself. She's beautiful, inside and out. Sensitive, creative, intelligent. Her dad has quit seeing her, period, since a few years ago. Doesn't call, doesn't acknowledge her birthday. Pays his support, but has cut off everything else. That affects everything she does. It affects how she perceives school, how she sees herself.

"I've felt rejection, too, and it's the most painful thing in the whole world. I don't want these kids to have that kind of pain. You know those pictures of kids starving in Africa, with the bones hanging out and all that? Our kids are internally starved. We don't see their ribs, but maybe we should look in their eyes."

Ley got up at this point in our conversation to retrieve a copy of the Sarah Scott yearbook from the shelf. She turned to a photograph of a seemingly happy, attractive child. "This is a picture of Carolyn," she said. "She looks like a normal kid, right? She's the most sexually abused little girl I've ever seen. But if you saw her, you'd think she's just a beautiful little girl. She's been put through it. She doesn't deserve to go through what she's going through. But she deserves people that care about her. She deserves every break she can get. She deserves this school. And she's making it.

"And my buddy Andrea, whose dad just left her. They don't deserve that, but they deserve somebody to listen to how they're hungry. It doesn't cost much to feed a kid by listening.

"Teachers should take an oath, just like a doctor. It's too easy to get a teaching degree. There's teachers out there that are doing it for ego reasons, or because of summer vacations. The reason you should be a teacher is kids. Bottom line: children. To give them a chance. If that's not what you're there for, get out of my way, because I don't want to be around you."

Creating a School-Community Partnership

In addition to her regular teaching responsibilities, Ley created and now coordinates an ambitious and highly successful school-community partnership program called Partners in Education. It brings adults from the business and professional world into the school to talk and work with students. In one five-month period alone—January to May 1992—there were ninety-two such events at Sarah Scott, including talks, workshops, and demonstrations by local lawyers, carpenters, chefs, bankers, Army officers, drug counselors, stockbrokers, potters, firefighters, meteorologists, prison guards, and artists.

"I found through listening to my students that a lot of them have no direction," Ley explained. "They don't understand why they're at school. If you ask them what would excite them to do in the future, what would they like to do beyond school, a lot of them would say, 'I dunno.' It's not even 'I don't know.' It's 'I dunno.' A large percentage come from single-parent homes, where the parents are barely making ends meet. Many are working for minimum wage."

Assistant Principal Kelley pointed out that many students do not have role models for postsecondary education. "Most of them have no idea that there is college or whatever beyond high school," she said. "They think if they get out of ninth grade they're doing well. Thus we developed our career awareness program, to help them explore the opportunities that are out there that they've never been exposed to."

To a great extent, the origins of the career awareness program can be traced to Ley's identification with and sense of responsibility for her students' development as human beings, not just art students. Ley attended Sarah Scott herself as a seventh and eighth grader, but her parents owned their own business. They could afford to take her to historic places, art museums, and other attractions all over the United States. Ley wanted to give her students the same advantages, so she created the partnership program.

Ley took advantage of an existing time slot that had been set aside for Team-Based Guidance, or TBG. She recognized that TBG was not working as intended. "Team-Based Guidance sounds great on paper," she said. "It's an administrative dream. It says, 'OK teachers—here's a half hour. Do something to help kids with life.' But some teachers just want to teach English or math—they don't want to do something different. I saw a lot of teachers just letting the kids study during TBG."

So Ley went around town and asked businesspeople to get involved in the schools. They were more than willing. She also discovered that, once she had organized the program, the other teachers would have to do little more than help with attendance. "It just freaks me out that schools are not doing this everywhere," Ley told us. "It's crazy. Everybody cries that they can't do anything because of the money. But it isn't money. It's a lack of innovation."

One of the most active participants in the program is Ivy Tech, Terre Haute's technical-vocational college. "I got Ivy Tech involved," Ley said, "because a lot of our students need to understand vocational schools. The thing that scares them is just entering the front door, finding where the school is. So every Tuesday fifteen of our students get a half day of actually being an Ivy Tech student, hands-on." Each student pays $1.50 for the bus, and they select which field they would like to look into, whether business and information systems, human services and health technologies, or applied arts and sciences, from welding to pollution control.

"Yesterday, the kids learned how to draw blood," she said. "They took cigarettes and put them in smoking machines to show how the tar would affect their lungs. I've never seen kids come back so excited. It doesn't cost the school anything, but it's really a good learning tool."

Another major player in the partnership is the nearby Regional Hospital. "They provide us with every different type of employee they have," said Ley, "from the person who answers the telephone right on up to the highest doctor. We go from the lowest-paid to the highest-paid person, and each one tells the kids what skills they need for their job and what courses in school will help them.

"You know who they enjoyed the most? Brenda McQueen—the lady who runs the hospital laundry. She got them excited about how she uses math to figure out how many sheets she washes each day, and how much detergent to use, and how hot the water has to be. And how with AIDS and other diseases it's even more important to get the right temperature to kill the germs. She really had these kids mesmerized. This woman had pride in her job as much as any doctor."

Ley gives Aballi credit for helping to make the partnership program work. "I've worked for three or four other principals in the last fourteen years," she said. "The great thing about working for Mr. Aballi is that he's not intimidated by an idea. Some principals will say, 'Somebody might not like this. Let's keep things calm.' Carlos says, 'Go for it. Good. It's your baby.' The caring and touching that happens in this school works because Carlos lets it work."

"You Can See How You're Affecting People's Lives"

Kenny started working as a volunteer in the pharmacy at Regional Hospital in June 1991, at the end of his seventh-grade year. It was a direct result of Ley's community partnership program with the hospital.

"I'd thought about volunteering at the hospital before," said Kenny, "but I didn't know how to go about it. Then this lady came to school as a guest speaker, and I called her that afternoon and she gave me the number of the lady in charge of volunteer services. She told me I could do it and sent me a form for my parents to sign."

Kenny's job involved processing faxed prescription orders from the various hospital wards and delivering medicines, I.V. units, and other materials to the nursing stations, then bringing back unused drugs, discharge fluids, and the like. He liked the work, liked the feeling of being a respected member of the hospital staff, and told us he was thinking of becoming a pharmacist "because you can see how you're affecting people's lives."

Kenny is studious—"I made top ten in academics last year," he said—friendly, talkative, a bit overweight, and not what some kids might describe as "cool." In a different school he might be considered a "nerd."

"Is it okay to be a smart kid in this school?" we asked him.

"Yeah," said Kenny. "I think so. I think most of the people here are smart."

Openness and Entrepreneurism

One of the most striking aspects of Sarah Scott Middle School is the openness—the willingness to talk honestly about important matters—of its staff and students. This quality is evident in virtually every encounter at Sarah Scott. When classes change and the halls are filled with students, all the teachers are outside their rooms, greeting and talking with kids. The kids obviously feel comfortable talking with adults, even visiting researchers and bigwigs from downtown.

Ramona Wedding, the assistant superintendent, described her astonishment at the directness of the Sarah Scott students during a visit to the school: "One boy, who later was identified as one of their biggest troublemakers, recognized me as someone from the central office. Again and again he asked me what could be done about the cafeteria menu. He didn't care about career choices or anything else. And to this very day that young man still speaks to me. I saw him at the mall just last week, and he praised me for putting a little variety in the cafeteria menu."

In fact, it was Aballi who was mainly responsible for improving the lunch scene. "When I arrived," he said, "you should have seen the cafeteria. The kids had no choice of what to eat. And it was depressing—dark and dingy. The whole room was lined with old freezers. The first thing I did was get rid of those freezers." At the time of our visits, the lunchroom was freshly painted, well lit, and decorated with student art.

Rewriting the menu was more complicated. The kitchen staff was at first reluctant to make changes because of the extra work involved, but Aballi was intent on upgrading not just the ambiance but also the nutritional quality of Sarah Scott's lunches. After listening to the cooks' point of view, he decided to change the schedule so that there would be only three lunch periods instead of four. This gave the kitchen staff more time between the waves of students to prepare a larger variety of items. The cafeteria now boasts a well-stocked and attractive salad bar.

The cafeteria story is an example of Aballi's willingness to tackle problems that other administrators might see as peripheral to the central issues of schooling. Aballi recognized that they are, in fact, critically important to the quality of life and human relationships in a school.

The story is also an example of Aballi's entrepreneurial spirit. In this case, he obtained the resources needed to install the salad bar and spruce up the lunchroom from the school district. But when the district is unresponsive or out of money, he still finds a way, often through outside grants and partnerships with civic and community groups and institutions, to get the job done.

The school's openness and entrepreneurial spirit may actually contribute to each other. Representatives of community groups feel welcome in the school and, as a result, offer their help more enthusiastically. Reciprocally, students and staff become more and more open to visitors, volunteers, and the larger world outside.

"One thing that just jumped out at me when I first started working here," said Theresa Haverkamp, Sarah Scott's at-risk counselor, "is that people just tell it like it is. They don't prance around and paint a rosy picture and tell you what you want to hear. They're very honest and open with the shortcomings, but they're also very proud and honest with the good things that are happening, too. You don't find that everywhere."

The honest communication at Sarah Scott has important implications for Haverkamp's work. Besides meeting with students individually and talking to health classes about violence, alcoholism, abusive relationships, and similar issues, she ran two support groups for children living with alcoholic adults.

"Kids identify themselves here," she told us. "They say, 'I've got this problem and I want some help with it.' I can't do that at my other school, because the kids are not willing. It's not a safe place to say, 'Yeah, you're right—my old man drinks too much,' or whatever. At my other school you have to dance around the problem, shroud it. They don't want anybody to know."

Seventh Grade: Portrait of a Team Leader

The twenty-nine students in the fifth-period world geography class were working in small groups under the direction of a visitor—Ken Horstman, the manager of a local restaurant chain who also volunteers, through the Terre Haute chapter of Junior Achievement, in Sarah Scott's Partners in Education program. He had assigned each group a problem from the real world of restaurant management. One group's problem: "Your best employees are leaving because a competitor is paying higher wages for shorter working hours." The kids were animatedly brainstorming solutions while Horstman moved around the room consulting.

After a few minutes the class reconvened and a spokesperson for this group reported its solution: pay higher wages. Another student commented, "But if we pay the workers more, we'll have less money for ourselves." The discussion then turned to working conditions and their relationship to job retention. The class's regular teacher, observing from the back of the room, commented that sometimes money is not the most important factor in a person's satisfaction with his or her job.

We asked this teacher (whom we will call Bob Highland because he asked us not to use his real name) about the class we had observed. Although career exploration is not exactly part of the standard world geography curriculum, he believes in its importance. "You have a businessman teaching business and economics at a seventh-grade level," Highland explained. "He told them what kinds of skills they should pick up in school. They can finally see a light at the end of the tunnel—why they're going through the educational process."

At the time of our visit, Highland taught world geography to the entire seventh grade—about 150 students in five classes. He also coached track and football and served as seventh-grade team leader, chairing the group's planning sessions and coordinating interdisciplinary units with the English teacher, Becky McElroy, the math teacher, Don Gosnell, and the science teacher, Theresa Adler.

On top of these responsibilities, Highland also had advisees, of course, with whom he met in the morning from 8:05 to 8:25. His load was barely manageable, and the advisory period was sometimes where theory crashed against reality. "I've been getting my kids ready for Geography Bowl [a countywide competition]," he told us, "so I haven't met with my advisory every day lately. I ship them out to other teachers twice a week. We've been practicing for the bowl in the morning. It's hard to find time to practice during the day or after school, so I just snag them in advisory."

Highland's colleagues and his principal all spoke glowingly of his abilities as a teacher and a team leader, but he continually pointed out flaws in his own work and public schools in general. It was not false modesty—he is just a naturally critical person who sees the unaddressed problems more clearly than the accomplishments.

"I see us stretched too thin," he told us, a comment that could be taken as a cry of both personal and institutional pain. "We have so many programs going on and we're going in so many different directions that sometimes you feel scatterbrained. I think we lose track of a lot of the average kids that have to go out in the workplace. We spend a lot of time with special ed and the top 5 percent, but the 80 percent in the middle are falling through the cracks."

Highland did not blame Aballi for the problems so much as the larger educational and political system. "Carlos has always taken care of me real well," he said. "Whenever I come in with a problem or concern, very seldom do I leave without it being rectified or without a promise of it being taken care of. But a lot of people who are in power, in a position to make decisions, don't have a clue of what effects they're going to have. They couldn't tell you much about what goes on on an average day at school. When they do come to us, a lot of times our advice is ignored.

"When Governor Bayh comes to Terre Haute, he doesn't come to our school. He comes to the school that places first in the math contest. People who have the power to make decisions are clueless when it comes to the average kid. I think they don't care, because if they did they'd come to these places. And I resent it. We're busting our butts to do a good job here, and we're not getting a lot of support from the people who could give it."

Highland leaned forward in his chair as he warmed to the subject. "For example," he said, "this building was built in 1917. We've got a school right down the road that's not even been here thirty years, and they're completely tearing it down—they're getting two gymnasiums, carpet, central air conditioning throughout. Look around: every junior high now is updated except ours. Have you been in our library? All they did was knock out a wall between two classrooms. We can't get state accredited because our library is not big enough.

"Our gym floor has three leaks in it. We had to stop a game about a month ago. What's that say to the kids when you go five miles down the street and they've got *two* gyms and they're tearing down a gym that's better than ours? What do you say to kids when they ask you, 'Why don't we get anything?'"

Highland was also critical of the teaming concept as practiced at Sarah Scott. It was a good idea, he acknowledged, to get groups of teachers to work together. "But at the same time," said the seventh-grade team leader, "it's divided us a little bit. It's almost team versus team versus team. We're not Sarah Scott Junior High so much as we're the seventh grade, or the eighth grade, or the ninth grade."

He talked about the difficulties of designing and teaching truly interdisciplinary units and maintained that the reality of teaming was not always what the theory promised. "Teaming was advertised as giving us flexible schedules where we could flip-flop kids," he said during one team meeting. "If you needed more than an hour, you could do it. That has not come to be. It's not as flexible as we were led to expect. I like the idea of having all the kids in common. But I don't like doing five geography classes a day for the rest of my days here. That would be what would get me to leave."

Teammate Becky McElroy is generally the one to put Highland's critiques in perspective. "I think you don't give yourself enough credit," she said to him, "and I think you are too hard on the team concept. You blame teaming for things that have nothing to do with teaming."

"Yeah," he admitted. "I might."

"We are empowered far more than a lot of teachers are," said McElroy, "and that's because of teaming."

"I'd go part way on that," Highland countered. "We are empowered, but it's not just teaming. It's the way the administration here at this school is."

"Carlos believes very strongly in the teaming concept," McElroy agreed. "He and I are working on a committee for the second phase of the Middle Grades Improvement Program. A couple of the other principals were talking about why they don't want any part of teaming. These same principals happen to be opposed to teacher empowerment, too. They believe that the principal should be the decision maker in all things. Carlos said to them—he was really worked up about this—when we team, those kids belong to those teachers. Those teachers own those kids. In his mind, they are our responsibility, and the decision making as far as the kids are concerned belongs to us."

The next morning, during its regular planning period, the seventh-grade team was making final plans for a geography competition in preparation for the district Geography Bowl. The assembly was being billed as the "Battle of the Sexes," with teams of boys competing against teams of girls.

McElroy looked uncomfortable. Finally she spoke up. "I have to say, something about this Battle of the Sexes is bothering me," she said. "Should we be pitting boys against girls? Should we be teaching them to compete with each other on the basis of gender?"

Highland groaned. "We've been planning this thing for a month," he complained, "and you bring this up the day before it's supposed to happen." Nevertheless, he agreed. "Battle of the Sexes" was out, and the competition became the "Academic Bowl" instead, with mixed teams of boys and girls working together.

"You Can Do It"

Consultants like Judy Johnston who have visited Sarah Scott invariably comment on the "traditional" style of the teachers. "I saw a lot of teachers sitting at their desks," Johnston reported. Many teachers did in fact arrange their rooms in neat rows of desks and stuck to a lecturing or question-and-answer format. But such outward appearances do not tell the whole story.

We saw good teaching and bad at Sarah Scott—as we did at every school. What most characterized this school was not ingenious curricula or especially skilled teachers; rather, it was the quality of teacher-student interactions. Teachers consistently built up their students instead of putting them down, encouraged their sense of efficacy, told them stories of their own lives and struggles, encouraged students to tell *their* own stories, and strove to make their students feel a vital connection among themselves and with the outside world.

Charles Shacklee teaches eighth-grade math at Sarah Scott. He is a quiet, balding man with a self-deprecating manner. The day of our visit, the topic was adding, subtracting, and multiplying positive and negative numbers, and the class was having trouble. A few of the students were obviously disengaged, sleepy, or perhaps just depressed. Others were trying hard but not understanding the material.

One girl was completely confused by the fact that four negative numbers multiplied together make a positive. Shacklee worked with her for at least five minutes, explaining the rule and then working the problem out the long way. She still did not get it. The other students were bored, but Shacklee never lost his patience. Instead, he decided to try another strategy.

To illustrate the concept of adding two negative numbers, Shacklee said he would bet Mary, who has a long, thick mane of dark hair, $30 that he had more hair on his head than she. All the kids laughed. This was clearly a losing proposition for the teacher. Then he bet Mary $60 that she had more facial hair than he. Another loser. "Okay," he said, "how much have I lost altogether?"

"Ninety dollars!" the whole class chimed in. Shacklee then wrote on the board: $(-30) + (-60) = -90$. "Did everyone follow?" he asked. Yes—they seemed to get it. "You're not dumb," he told them. "You can do it. Some of this is hard to soak in," he said. "It was for me. We'll review it two or three times till you get it."

Later in that same class period Shacklee announced that there would be a "surprise pop quiz" the next day. The students objected: "It's not a pop quiz if we know in advance!" Shacklee smiled. "If we pass," he said, "we can get doughnuts. If we pass with a C-plus average, we can have lots of doughnuts. But if one person doesn't pass, then no doughnuts. So I trust you'll study and help your friends."

After class, we mentioned that this seemed to be a challenging group to work with. Shacklee took this as a criticism of the kids and instantly came to their defense, pointing out how hard they worked and how good they were. He is simply not one of those teachers who puts students down or stands by when others do it. His kids, in turn, are utterly devoted to him.

Seventh-grade general science teacher Theresa Adler had just finished giving her students a quiz on recycling and the environment. After they had graded their own papers in class, she asked, "How many of you got four or more right?" Most of the students raised their hands. "Okay," she said, "do you guys know that you did better than the average American adult? Do you see that you're getting smarter than the people out there that are older than you? So you have to educate all those old fogies in the world."

Later in that same class, Adler took ten minutes to describe in minute detail her recent vacation. She knew that many of her students had never seen the ocean or traveled far beyond the boundaries of Terre Haute, for that matter.

"I went to Florida last week," she said, "and I want to share this with you because when I was young my family didn't take a lot of vacations. But I like to go different places and see different things." The class was absolutely still, listening.

"One of the things I did when I was down there was something I have always wanted to do but never done," she said. "I went snorkeling." The students exclaimed, asked questions, talked to each other all at once. The teacher let the buzz go on for a moment, then continued. She described the boat, the ocean, the breathing apparatus, the process of getting into the water, and the coral reef with great vividness. She talked about her own apprehension, her own moment of panic at getting a mouthful of salt water, and her feeling of exaltation at the beauty of the reef. The students were there with her, in the blue-green water.

Eighth-grade team leader Tom Taylor—a fast-talking, super-confident, old-fashioned teacher—embodies the complex reality of change and development in the middle grades. "There is still in all of us, including me, a good deal of traditionalism that is hard for us to throw off," Taylor said. "I thought I would be the hardest to change because I'm the old dog that's been at it too long. I was against teaming. 'Prove to me that it will work,' I said. Well, we proved it ourselves.

"It's not the answer to everything, but it works, especially with new teachers. I've been here twenty years. I remember when I first started teaching, this place was an absolute zoo. Our kids were ten times harder than we have today. Gosh, it was awful. I needed help, and nobody could help me. I had to learn by myself.

"People are all scared of change. Teachers have developed a system to cope—not necessarily to educate, but to cope. Carlos wanted us to change teaching styles and do more interdisciplinary things, and our teachers went to him and said, 'We're not ready for it. We're old, traditional teachers and we're simply not ready.' And I told him, 'If you push it, you're going to lose teaming. Leave it alone.' So he did what was best. He listened.

"He took us to all kinds of interdisciplinary workshops, and I kept saying, 'We're not ready yet.' Well, this year we got ready. But we did it because we chose to do it. And not all my teachers chose to do it, so I left them out.

"I'm traditional. My best method of teaching is lecture. I'm banging desks. I'm like a Southern Baptist preacher. That's what I'm good at. I tell stories. We're the only culture in the world that doesn't have any stories. If you use storytelling in your teaching, you don't need that god-awful textbook." Interestingly, though Taylor describes himself as an old-fashioned lecture-style teacher, he has his students using computers to draw Civil War battlefield maps.

We asked Taylor what had changed most at Sarah Scott in the past few years. "Carlos has brought us a positive attitude," he told us. "He drags us and pushes us. He says, 'Let's try it. If it doesn't work, we'll punt.' And he's never said no. Well, one time he said no, and we did it anyway. We take kids on airplane trips. He said, 'You can't pull this off.' But we did it."

His team's trips to Detroit and St. Louis, planned by Taylor and assistant team leader Lori Routh, were indeed the talk of the eighth grade. The entire grade was engrossed (some said obsessed) with fundraising campaigns that he had organized to help pay the air fares. For most of the students, it was their first flight. These airplane trips, like almost everything at Sarah Scott, fit into a larger vision: Taylor was determined to help his kids fly—figuratively and literally.

A Mixed Picture at District Headquarters

It is hard to judge, based on our observations, whether progress at Sarah Scott was, in the last analysis, helped or hindered by policies and practices in the central office downtown. The picture was certainly mixed.

Some Sarah Scott staff members were outspokenly critical of the district leadership. The Middle Grades Improvement Program aimed at districtwide change; it required all six Vigo County junior highs to coordinate their plans for the continuing use of the endowment's discretionary funds. But three years into the program, when Sarah Scott's MGIP Advisory Committee was ready with its proposals for additional staff development and other programs, the other schools were still carrying out basic needs assessments. Critical time and opportunities were lost, committee members said, while the other schools got their acts together.

One outspoken teacher complained that the district level steering committee wasted three long meetings rewriting its one-paragraph mission statement "which was fine to begin with." He attributed the problem to central office indifference and ignorance about "what's going on out here." And when Aballi, as chairman of the district curriculum committee, tried to push the other junior high school principals to consider reform ideas, he was met with open hostility. "There has been some resentment from my colleagues," Aballi admitted, "because I questioned the way things were done in the past."

"Some people saw Carlos as a wimp because he was the first to eliminate corporal punishment," said Assistant Superintendent Wedding, one of the few district level administrators who praised Aballi's work. "He wasn't seen as macho, because he wasn't going to beat the kids. He was going to talk with them and see what the problem was."

Where, then, did Sarah Scott fit into the district's picture? When we talked with Charles M. Clark, Vigo County's school superintendent, he did not single out Sarah Scott School or Carlos Aballi as leaders or exemplars in the movement toward successful middle school education in Terre Haute. Clark did pay tribute to the obvious change among the students at Sarah Scott. "They have much more pride in their school than they had a few years ago," he said, "much more feeling of solidarity." And he mentioned the adviser-advisee program as a specific strength. But when we pressed him to compare Sarah Scott with the other junior highs, he was noncommittal: "I think, for a traditional building, they've come along real well."

The district's initial approach to the Middle Grades Improvement Program was to let each school determine its own priorities—to be independent. "One of the things that we attempted to do with MGIP," said Superintendent Clark, "was to allow each school a great deal of flexibility in how they would use the funds, what they would put their emphasis on. I think that was probably wise, because you have to begin somewhere. We didn't say, 'This is the agenda and everybody will march in step to this kind of a drummer.'"

But there is a fundamental difference between this kind of laissez-faire administration and Aballi's philosophy of "Go for it—it's your baby." While Aballi was more than willing to listen and to let his staff try new ideas, his own commitment to reform was rock-hard, and his values and priorities were never obscure. Until the arrival of Ramona Wedding, no such clear direction appears to have come from the central office.

Wedding took over as assistant superintendent in 1991, and many Sarah Scott staff members felt that she had made a real difference. "Her support of middle-level practices has been outstanding," Aballi told us, "and she has required all the junior high principals to begin planning for the implementation of interdisciplinary teams beginning with the 1993–94 school year."

At the same time, Aballi is the first to say that the district's attitude of "Do what you want—just don't screw up" gave him enough freedom to make real changes within his own school. A more aggressively directive central administration might have actually been worse for Sarah Scott than a hands-off regime.

Effects of the Lilly Initiative at Sarah Scott

The transformation of Sarah Scott Middle School illustrates the potentially profound influence of an external change agent like the Lilly Endowment's Middle Grades Improvement Program on an individual school, even where the central office administration is indifferent or preoccupied with other matters. Carlos Aballi is certainly an essential element of the Sarah Scott story, but his efforts, and those of other critical staff members like Mary Ley and Judy Elsey, were inspired and supported in numerous large and small ways by the Lilly Endowment staff and its programs. We strongly doubt that the school would look and feel the way it does today without MGIP.

The list of the endowment's influences is long: Aballi's exposure to middle school research and theory as a Lilly Fellow; the full faculty participation in the MGAP self-assessment process; staff development funds for advisory training, cooperative learning, affective education, and interdisciplinary teaching; the school's participation in the endowment's Reading and Writing in the Disciplines (REWIND), Reading for Real, and Teachers Under Cover programs; and support for school-community links like the Partners in Education program and the school's Homework Hotline.

"Probably the best thing that came through the Lilly money was the workshops where we learned new and different teaching strategies," said Lana Shuck, the parenting and child development teacher. Mary Ley described a powerful secondary effect of Lilly's attention: a sense of being valued. "The change here is partly Carlos," she said, "but it's also the Lilly funding. The staff development money has made it so teachers can have meetings in a respectable place, with nice meals. That makes us feel like we're equal to other schools, that we're treated with dignity. The Lilly name in this town means everything. It means respect. It means dignity. It means class."

The endowment's commitment to the school continues: in 1992 Sarah Scott won a major grant in the Lilly-sponsored Indiana School Guidance and Counseling Leadership Project. A team of counselors and teachers met regularly during the 1991–92 school year to develop a comprehensive proposal to strengthen the career guidance and advisory programs and to foster better home-school relations, especially with families of low-achieving students. Their proposal was one of just seven winners out of those submitted by twenty-five schools and school districts statewide who had been invited to participate. And in the winter of 1994, Sarah Scott received one of twelve School Recognition Grants to continue to deepen and extend its reform efforts in the coming years.

Change Is Never-Ending

We visited Sarah Scott in the spring of 1992, when the Guidance and Counseling Committee was in the midst of its work. It had already identified the weak spots in the school's program to be highlighted in its proposal to Lilly: parent involvement, the advisory program, career guidance. Aballi also spoke candidly with us about other problems: inadequate planning time for teachers, staff members feeling overloaded and overwhelmed by the stress of change, the need to improve classroom instruction, and the still-high student suspension rate.

Aballi admitted that the last of these items was probably the most intractable, and he related it to the community's long-held belief in corporal punishment. "We have not made great strides in the area of discipline," he said. "While the staff has accepted the no-paddling policy, we are still too punitive minded. We have not been very effective in changing that attitude."

"We're working on it," he reported in a follow-up conversation at the start of the 1992–93 school year. "We're doing some preventive work with certain staff members to try to head off problems before they become suspensions." He had reassigned Sandra Kelley, an administrator with obvious skills in relating to students, to take responsibility for discipline and had arranged for training in new cooperative techniques. And plans had been laid for doing away with the on-site suspension room entirely.

In every other problem area as well, Aballi had taken some action. To improve home-school relations, he had set aside Wednesday morning advisory periods for parents to come talk with teachers and arranged for them to be able to stay afterward and have breakfast. The school also sponsored panel discussions for parents on issues related to behavior problems and living with young adolescents. A new parent advisory council was also taking shape, and the school had opened a new parents' room—the old teachers' smoking lounge. ("We now have no teachers who smoke," Aballi reported.)

These actions began to pay off in dramatic ways during the 1993–94 school year. Though Aballi was no longer at Sarah Scott (he had been reassigned as principal of the Honey Creek Middle School in Terre Haute), the school was thriving under the principalship of Kelley, the former assistant principal. Kelley reports that parental involvement has exploded, with between 100 and 125 parents actively working to improve the school. School events and performances are standing-room-only. Close to 1,500 people showed up for one concert in the fall, though Kelley thinks that might have had something to do with the fact that there was an Elvis impersonator on the program.

Other changes were put in motion after our 1992 visits to the school. To encourage more cross-grade sharing of ideas on curriculum and instruction, the seventh- and eighth-grade teams had scheduled joint planning meetings. The fine arts, practical arts, and physical education teachers' schedules were rearranged to allow them to meet at least some of the time with the core subject teacher teams. The school had also begun to implement a new "inclusion" program that integrated students with disabilities in regular classrooms.

To improve the guidance program and smooth the transition from middle school to high school, Aballi had arranged for the entire high school counseling staff to visit Sarah Scott and talk with the students. A new program was being developed to help students plan for careers in the next century. And Aballi had arranged to take some of his staff on a winter retreat to talk about stress caused by change in the workplace. There was not a single item that we or others had identified as a problem needing attention at Sarah Scott that Aballi—and then Kelley—had not taken some concrete action to address.

Though it is still too early to say for sure, we suspect that Sarah Scott Middle School will pass with flying colors the hardest test of school reform: sustained improvement even after the departure of a wonderful principal. In the last analysis, the critical element of change is not the man or woman at the top. It is the quality of relationships between people throughout the school.

Chapter Three

Making Connections

These kids become tough because that is what the
law of poverty and violence on the street dictates.
Underneath it all, they are hurting.
—*from the journal of Elizabeth Wiley,*
student teacher, Harshman School

Only if I had a face to show you what's Inside
To show I am Something . . .
A Somebody
While I'm still on this Earth I have a beautiful
Inside Face.
—*Semorris Moore, student, Harshman School*

H. L. Harshman Junior High School (now Middle School) was an
extremely poor, inner-city school in downtown Indianapolis. Under
the leadership of Principal Marcia Capuano, faculty and community members began to take a closer look at the "inside faces" of
students and to understand the additional burden that urban life
places on these young adolescents. Through a comprehensive program that addressed students' physical, emotional, and intellectual
needs, Harshman brought new hope to its students, their families,
and the surrounding community. Its story demonstrates what can
happen when faculty and community, undaunted by the complexity of the problems that face them, join hands to bring about social
change.

The Full-Service School

From the outside, Harshman Junior High, also known as School
101, is featureless. The two-story, light-colored, rectangular building looks like many other junior high schools built in the late

1950s. Traffic rushes by on 10th Street, the wide avenue that fronts the school. Inside, a calm and orderly atmosphere prevails, one that was not here several years ago when Nancy Reagan and other dignitaries visited the school to rail against drugs and violence. There are many signs of pride: "READ" appears in bold letters over the drinking fountain, students' poetry and project work line the hallways and stairwells, and the bulletin board proclaims "Harshman and the Community Working Hand in Hand."

In 1991–92, approximately half of the 780 students at Harshman were African American; the other half were white. By almost any economic measure, it was the poorest school in Indiana. Fully 90 percent of the students qualified for free or reduced lunches, and many of their parents were on welfare or working at minimum-wage jobs. For many years, Harshman students had the lowest test scores in the state. The surrounding community, known as the Near East Side, has encountered serious problems over the past twenty years as its industrial base has eroded. Family and student health problems are widespread, and family violence and youth gangs are not uncommon. The neighborhood has the highest crime rate in the city, and nearly a hundred Harshman students were on probation or parole from the juvenile justice system during the 1991–92 school year. All of these factors have helped give Harshman a reputation as a "bad" school.

When Capuano arrived as Harshman's principal in 1990, the school had experienced seven principals in five years. Some could not deal with the stress of working with students with such severe and complex needs, while others viewed Harshman as a way station on the road to more enviable professional positions. Historically, the school had a high burnout rate among both administrators and teachers. One-third of the staff left every year. Complicating this picture, within Capuano's first year, Indianapolis Public Schools (IPS) had a serious budget shortfall that caused widespread layoffs. As a result, nearly half of Harshman's staff received reassignments. But Capuano was not easily discouraged.

Unlike her predecessors, she was excited by the opportunities she saw at the school and immediately introduced major changes.

Capuano brought with her the conviction that, in addition to being literate, young people need to be physically, socially, and emotionally healthy. She envisioned a comprehensive, full-service school that would be the centerpiece of the local community, offering a range of educational, physical and mental health, and social services to young people and their families. "Education involves everything," said Capuano. "It's like a piece of fabric and the threads intertwine."

If she had her way, schools would offer families "one-stop shopping" for all their medical, educational, and social service needs. Capuano feels that so long as schools rely on a patchwork of community agencies and organizations for services, they will be underserved. "As long as these services are provided in different organizations, there will always be problems due to different organizational structures, turf issues, confidentiality problems, and differing policies and procedures," she argues.

Capuano is a woman with an iron will, driven by an intense commitment to serve young people. She is not a charismatic leader; she does not stand out in a crowd. In fact, Capuano seems almost shy and reserved upon first meeting. She holds herself erect, walks slowly, speaks softly, and is always very much in control. A hard worker (ten- and twelve-hour days are typical), she lets nothing stand in the way of her objectives. "That woman is made of steel inside," said Marty Miles, a local community leader. "Her strength is unbelievable. She may be set back, but she does not stop."

Acting swiftly after her arrival, Capuano's first major initiative was to institute a host of new physical and mental health services for her students. Next, she introduced a wide array of reading initiatives, recognizing that, without reading skills, students would have difficulty mastering other school subjects. And finally, she set about strengthening the ties between Harshman and the local community and building community support for her programs. Each of these three areas was a critical cornerstone in her comprehensive plan for school improvement.

Capuano's greatest strength in carrying out these initiatives was her ability to identify resources and mobilize them to action. Never a solo player, she sought help from community leaders, parents, and teachers seeking to make a difference. She reinvigorated the school improvement committee and the recently formed school-community council. With their support, she eliminated student tracking by ability group and assigned all teachers and students to seven "houses" or teams. Using data to document various problems, she then sought faculty and community assistance, as well as external funding, in solving them.

The School Health Clinic

As soon as Capuano arrived at Harshman, she identified health services as a critical need. "Many of the students would have their heads on their desks, complained about feeling ill, or didn't look like they felt well," she said. Attendance records showed that many students were absent from school for long periods of time, often because of recurring illnesses. Harshman students suffered from a number of chronic health problems, the result of poor nutrition and health habits. The school had a low daily attendance record: an average of 79 percent compared to 90.5 percent for the district as a whole. These numbers were especially troubling to Capuano, who recognized the close relationship between good health and education. "We, as educators, know that the physical and emotional needs of students must be addressed before we can focus a student's total attention on the task of acquiring knowledge," she explained. "How can students learn if they're not in school or if they're in class but not feeling well?"

Additional research confirmed that students at Harshman were medically underserved. Survey results revealed that most students were not getting the services they needed, in part because their parents tended to focus on the younger children in the family first and in part because parents were preoccupied with providing other basics such as food and shelter. Although People's Health Center, which is located just down the street from Harshman, offered low-cost medical services, nearly two in five students who were sick during the year did not receive medical attention. Students explained that their parents were unwilling to leave work to take them to a doctor, lacked transportation, or did not believe they were ill. According to Capuano, "Many students were sent to school when they were ill because parents consider the school a primary source of assistance regardless of the area of need."

Armed with this information, Capuano, together with Pat Kiergan, the IPS nursing supervisor, and other district staff, began to explore ways of creating a health clinic at Harshman, using the successful clinic at nearby Arsenal Technical High School as a model. Dr. Charlene Graves, director of the Pediatric Residency Program at Methodist Hospital and founder of the Arsenal Tech clinic, was generous in sharing advice, as were the staff at People's. The major hurdle was obtaining the funds necessary to support the clinic's staff and equipment.

In the summer of 1991, Johnson & Johnson invited Indianapolis and several other cities across the country to submit proposals to set up health clinics for young adolescents under the auspices of the Community Health Care Program. This was just the opportunity that Capuano and others in the community had been looking for. Working in close collaboration with IPS, the Methodist Hospital of Indiana, People's Health Center, and the Marion County Health Department, they submitted a proposal to develop a full-service clinic at Harshman. With a $30,000 grant from Johnson & Johnson and additional support from Methodist Hospital and the Drug Free Schools and Communities program, the clinic opened its doors in November 1991.

"To get a service up and running in three months is really fairly amazing," said Heliene Houdek, project director for the clinics at both Arsenal Tech and Harshman. "The Tech experience was invaluable—you couldn't have done it without experienced people who knew what needed to be done."

Today the Harshman Health Clinic provides an array of services to students: physical examinations, immunizations, and assessment and treatment of common illnesses. The first school-based clinic in the state of Indiana at the middle-grades level, it has been hugely successful. In its first six months of operation, the clinic diagnosed and treated approximately 280 Harshman students. In 1991–93, nearly four hundred students scheduled appointments, and many more were seen on an emergency basis.

On a typical Monday morning, we observed a group of youngsters congregate outside the clinic, which consists of a tiny office and two small examining rooms located just across the hall from the principal's office. The students were waiting patiently to see Lori Rhegness, the clinic's nurse practitioner, who, with the help of a licensed practical nurse, staffed the clinic for five hours a day, four days a week. The staff were supported by an on-call physician at People's, and Graves donated her time at Harshman one morning a month.

Eighth grader Tenille was one of the first students in the clinic that morning, looking for relief from an ear infection. "I came and sat here today because this morning, when I woke up, my ears were puffy," she said. "I never had a health clinic in my school before. It's real convenient."

Tenille was one of twenty-seven students seeking assistance from the clinic staff that Monday, typically the busiest day of the week. Characteristic student ailments include intestinal and skin problems, sore throats, lice, burns, ringworm, conjunctivitis, and inadequate nutrition. The clinic also sees a fair number of students with stomach and headaches, cuts, and bruises. Virtually all of the clinic's services are free, although students who can afford it are asked to pay $5 for their annual sports physical. The Methodist Hospital Task Force, an auxiliary run by physicians' spouses, provides free medicine to needy students.

"Our goal is providing health education for the children and getting them the follow-up care that they don't usually receive," said Rhegness. "We figure that if we can treat common illnesses while they're in school, it will save them from having to miss school to see the doctor. It will also eliminate parents' waiting until tomorrow or the day after. Adolescents are going through so many changes in their bodies," she added. "The clinic gives them somebody who can look at what's bothering them and say, 'You're okay.' Or somebody to give them medicine and say, 'This is what's wrong with you. You'll be okay.' A lot of these kids need reassurance, 'cause many of them don't get the attention they need at home."

The nurse schedules students without a temperature to return at a less busy time. Scheduled appointments teach responsibility and give the staff time to deal with more serious cases without being continually interrupted. If students need emergency treatment, they are worked into the schedule. Students requiring more complex treatment are referred by the center to other agencies, including neighboring health centers and local hospitals.

"The school health clinic has two primary benefits," explained Rhegness. "The first is that the health services are here and available when the kids need them. Many of the students didn't receive services before, either because they weren't affordable or because their problems seemed to get better over time—like ear infections. But these can become chronic if they aren't picked up, and they can do a lot of damage if they aren't dealt with immediately.

"The other aspect of having the health center here is to give students some long-term skills for dealing with their health needs and making more appropriate health decisions in the future. I think the two are very closely intertwined. You develop trust by meeting someone's immediate needs. Then, they'll be more apt to seek appropriate medical attention in the future." She added, "I think the clinic works because it's for them. It's not for their parents— it's not for their little brothers and sisters. It's to meet their needs."

The health clinic requires that each student have a parent consent form on file in order to receive treatment. And, while parents and siblings may not use the clinic's services directly, educating parents about proper health care is an important goal. Soon after the clinic opened, for example, Harshman experienced a widespread outbreak of conjunctivitis, a particularly virulent strain that could have led to serious eye problems if left untreated. The clinic contacted parents to warn them of how contagious the strain was and to offer tips on how to prevent it from spreading. "Make sure your child washes her hands, use separate towels, have your child use her own makeup," staff said. Rhegness added, "Parents are very thankful you're doing something for them. They let us know how great it is to be able to have us down here."

Like other school-based services across the country, the Harshman Health Clinic is sensitive to community concerns and expectations in the area of sex education. "One of the difficulties in terms of prevention of future pregnancies is that many of the girls don't have a very good sense of self," said Houdek. "Because of that they don't protect themselves from circumstances that put them at risk." The school uses the Choice curriculum, intended to help students make wiser decisions about daily health matters, including prevention of pregnancy and sexually transmitted diseases.

If students report that they are sexually active, the Harshman clinic refers them to family planning services at People's Health Center. The Harshman Health Clinic also conducts free pregnancy tests on request. If the test is positive, students are given one day to tell their parents so that they can make informed decisions about the future. If students are unable or unwilling to tell parents on their own, the clinic staff will assist them. On request, clinic staff also help families arrange prenatal care for their youngsters at either People's or a private hospital of their choice. People's runs a comprehensive prenatal program for young mothers, including regular prenatal checkups and parent education courses.

Harshman also provides two weekly support groups, one for youngsters who are pregnant and one for youngsters with newborns.

According to Capuano, "While both groups are labeled 'young mothers,' their needs are quite different. Each group responds to the needs and concerns of the kids themselves." Pregnant girls need help in getting along with friends and family, eating right, and general health care. Once the baby is born, the group's focus shifts to parenting skills and dealing with the issues surrounding parenthood.

In its first two years of operation, the clinic staff and supervising physicians met with Harshman administrators once a month to talk about the clinic's progress. Out of these sessions came ideas for expanding services and finding permanent funding. When the Johnson & Johnson grant ran out, People's Health Center decided to fund the school-based program, thereby extending existing services to young adolescents. Operating under People's umbrella, the clinic has added a social worker who makes home visits to young mothers, works with drug-affected youth, and provides other needed services. With a full-time nurse on-site five days a week and a part-time nurse practitioner, the program is stronger than ever. Capuano noted with pride, "We've gone from soft money to hard money." In the world of pilot programs, getting permanent funding is all too rare.

The Student Assistance Program

In addition to opening a health clinic, Harshman has developed a comprehensive Student Assistance Program (SAP) to help meet students' social and emotional needs. In August 1991, Harshman served as a pilot junior high school for the new program, which was initiated by IPS in an effort to pool resources more effectively. The original SAP team consisted of a coordinator, two Harshman social workers, two guidance counselors, selected teachers, and the health clinic staff. In preparing for the program, Capuano and the SAP staff received three weeks of intensive training at St. Paul's Hospital, a highly respected prevention training center in Milwaukee.

The SAP's original focus was on drug counseling, helping students who are affected by their own drug use or someone else's. Since its inception, the program has expanded to encompass other student needs and concerns, including separation and divorce, death and loss, decision making, self-esteem, and conflict resolution. There are also programs for young mothers and students recently released from treatment centers. Weekly support groups form the core of the program.

Kris Clerkin, the SAP coordinator, works at Harshman several days a week. She meets with the SAP team once a week to share information, exchange notes, and discuss the best approach to various problems. "It's a team effort," said Clerkin.

Students are referred to SAP by teachers, peers, parents, or themselves. The first thing the team does is a preliminary assessment. "Once we've gathered all the information," said Clerkin, "we bring it to the core team meeting and figure out together what might be most beneficial for the student. Then we place them under the SAP umbrella, perhaps by assigning them to one of several ongoing programs—individual counseling, social services, or a conflict management group. Or we might decide that the child needs to be tested for special education or referred to a community agency. What's done depends on the child's needs."

The Concerned Others is an SAP group designed for students who are affected by someone else's chemical dependency. It allows students to explore their feelings, become better informed, and learn coping strategies. "In most cases, they can't talk to anyone at home about their feelings and concerns, because the problem is denied," explained Clerkin. "It's like the big family secret. They need some safe place where they can start to express their anger, their fear, their feeling of powerlessness." The group helps youngsters talk about their feelings and recognize that they are normal. It teaches youngsters that alcoholism is a disease. Most important, the group lets kids know that they do have power, at least over themselves, and provides them with a number of safe coping techniques.

The Conflict Management Group, another SAP initiative, helps students look at alternative ways to handle daily conflicts. Peter, a tall, sandy-haired seventh grader, was a member of the first Conflict Management Group, and volunteered to run a second. "We all suspected our teachers of throwing us in there because of our behavior in class," he said. "I got suspended early in the year for beating the crap out of one kid. They helped us deal with conflicts and fighting. How to be friends with them instead of wiping them up and down the floors. Listen to other people's opinions before you go off the hook. We did a little role playing, a lot of talking." When asked what motivated him to volunteer for a second group, Peter offered this rationale: "There's too many people getting shot and killed over dope, drugs, shoes, hats, jackets, and pants. It's just too much. So, maybe I thought I could help do something with just a small group."

Sometimes the SAP staff invites community members to visit and share their expertise. The Choice program, organized and directed by staff from the local mental health department, is a prime example. It tackles different topics each week, including self-esteem, sexuality, decision making, and drugs and alcohol.

For Crystal, one of nine students who participated in the initial Choice program, the most beneficial aspect of the weekly meetings was the opportunity to discuss sensitive issues with peers. "It's one thing to think you're going against the crowd," she said. "It's another when you're part of the crowd."

By all accounts, the SAP at Harshman has been highly successful. In its very first semester, the program provided one or more support groups for approximately two hundred students. In 1992–93, approximately 320 students participated in twenty-five different support groups. "We've received positive comments from the kids themselves, which makes us feel really good," said Clerkin. "It's a new program, and we've moved very slowly. But I now have kids coming to me and asking me if they can be in groups. Self-referral is the most promising thing; it's where we want to get to."

Of course, not all referrals come from students themselves. Some come from the health clinic, which finds itself on the front line in identifying students' emotional and social problems. "Some kids come down here for a stomach ache, which turns out to be negative," said Rhegness. "I'll ask them, 'Well, is there anything going on at home?' I had a kid tell me, 'Oh yeah, everything's all messed up. My dad's trying to take my brother out of the house; my mom's on medication for this or that,' and on and on."

Other referrals to the SAP come from classroom teachers, who play an important role in helping students find words for their feelings. The honesty and expressiveness of Harshman students can be stunning, as in the following poems:

> My life walks over little problems
> The big ones become mounds of trouble
> Like a puzzle with a missing piece
> I am missing my dad
> Wondering where he is . . .
> and when this pain will end.

> Sharonda Celestine

My Dad

> He comes and goes every
> two years
> He stops to see me and
> takes me out to eat
> He takes me to his family
> to see how they are
> He comes and goes every
> two years.

> Tim Lee

Reading at Harshman: The Key to Academic Success

At the same time that efforts to address students' physical and emotional needs were under way, Marcia Capuano sought to improve Harshman's academic life. Her first priority was helping students with reading. When she took over as principal, 75 percent of the students were in the bottom quartile in reading on standardized tests. Knowing that poor reading skills slow down performance in other disciplines, the faculty initiated a number of programs designed to promote reading across the curriculum.

At first the reading program focused almost exclusively on making books available to youngsters, motivating them to read, and providing multiple opportunities for sustained silent reading. Then Capuano added a staff development program aimed at helping teachers of all subjects support their students' reading skills. Today there are at least twelve different components to the reading program, which receives much of its funding from the Middle Grades Reading Improvement Program, funded in 1989 by the Lilly Endowment to address the unmet reading needs of Indiana's young adolescents.

Personalizing Reading

When we entered the school library, we found vivacious Sandy Nolan, Harshman's library/media specialist, busily sorting books alongside a number of adult and student volunteers. The library itself was full of neatly ordered shelves and comfortable reading tables. But, as Nolan was quick to point out, most of the reading at Harshman does not occur in this room. Rather, under a program called Reading Excitement and Paperbacks (REAP), Nolan has brought the library to the classroom.

REAP was developed by Jack Humphrey of Evansville, whose Reading Network has brought many creative reading programs to

Indiana. According to Nolan, "All of the research says that if you have silent sustained reading three to five times a week, reading scores improve. Yet kids can't all come to the library—it's not big enough. And we found that even when they did come on a regular basis, they still never got to class with their books. So we decided to bring the books to them."

Nolan reads nonstop during the summer to find books her students will like. She also asks their preferences among books, TV shows, movies, and music as a guide to their interests. "If you give kids books they don't like, they won't read them," she said. "I tell them from the beginning, 'You're a reader now. If you don't like a book, it's okay. Get another one. It's like watching TV—you can always switch channels and find something you like better.'"

Once the books are selected, she and her volunteer staff choose the titles and make crates available for teachers, with approximately forty books in each crate. The crates rotate from class to class. In a typical year, almost seven thousand books are out of the library being used by students. Nolan admitted that she loses a lot of books this way, but she believes it is a wonderful problem to have. "I've been praying for the day that books would be stolen," she said. "That means they're now considered valuable."

Tag Team Reading

One of the most popular reading programs at Harshman is called Tag Team Reading, organized by Nolan every six weeks. On Tag Team Reading day, seventy students—ten from each of the seven Harshman units or houses—are chosen to participate.

We witnessed Tag Team Reading during our visit. As soon as the first period bell rang, all seventy kids eagerly crowded into the library. Nolan welcomed them, gave them their instructions, and introduced the book she had selected for the day's event: *Strange Attraction*, a science fiction novel by William Sleator. Then all but seven of the students returned to their regular classes. Those who remained picked up their copies of the paperback, took their assigned seats, quietly opened their books, and began to read.

About thirty minutes later, these readers were joined by another seven students. Teammates spent a few moments whispering to one another, with the first reader bringing the second up to date in the story. Then the first group of students returned to class while their replacements picked up where they had left off in the book.

Exchanges like these continued throughout the day. At the end of the day, all seventy kids returned to the library where, as teams, they took a test on what they had read. Although the winning team got a book, all participants received a certificate and a special prize.

"We enjoy this activity the most," said Nolan. "Kids read all day long, and teachers talk to them about their reading. 'What did you think of this? Where are you in the book?' It's motivating for the teachers as well as the students. We've got seven teams, one for each house. Seventy kids in here at once all talking about a book. They're all good—they're just real good."

Junior Readers

The Junior Readers program combines two of Harshman's primary goals: it strengthens students' reading skills and links Harshman with the surrounding community. Junior Readers, as many as thirty to forty-five students on a given day, visit local elementary schools and read to the younger children. In 1991–92, the Junior Readers made six visits, but the program has become so popular that additional elementary schools have requested Junior Readers.

All the junior readers are volunteers, and they represent a variety of different cultures, backgrounds, and achievement levels. Nolan encourages all students to get involved and has very few requirements for participation. "They have to be responsible enough to come in and get a permission slip and turn it in," she said. "Then they have to be responsible enough to come and practice reading their material on a regular basis. If they can't do that, then they don't go."

To ensure the program's success, Nolan leaves little to chance. She assigns each student to an elementary class, arranges transportation, accompanies students to their destinations, and carefully prepares them for their visits.

"I try to match the reader with an appropriate age group," she said. "Some want to read to sixth graders, but most like reading to younger children. We also read to the special education classes.

"The first time, I help the kids choose what to read. After they've had some guidance, they can choose on their own. We also talk about how to read aloud, what little kids like, and what to expect. When the kids get there and they read aloud, they get so much glory from it. And the little kids—they think they're wonderful."

Even students who have difficulty reading can serve as Junior Readers. "I work with them," said Nolan. "I listen to them, and they also practice with their classroom teachers. It's been wonderfully successful. They feel comfortable with their story before they go over there, and they just love it. It's another way to involve them in reading. Seeing the children's joy after they've done what they've done is lovely."

Teachers Under Cover

To motivate students further, teachers at Harshman are also involved in their own reading program called Teachers Under Cover— another innovation of Jack Humphrey that was funded by the Lilly Endowment. Teachers who wish to participate belong to one of two reading groups; each selects a book to read and discuss. Then they exchange books with the other group.

Harshman teachers make a special point of letting students know that they read for pleasure. Participating faculty members have Teacher Under Cover sweatshirts that they wear on book discussion day. According to Susan Avery, an eighth-grade language arts teacher, "It's always good for the students to see that teachers themselves are interested in the written word."

Teachers select the books they're interested in reading, and their choices are pretty eclectic. One year, the teachers read *The Dumbing of America*, a few popular novels including *Possession* and *Fried Green Tomatoes*, Erma Bombeck's new book, and Katherine Hepburn's autobiography, *Me*.

Avery said that what the teachers choose to read is less important than the act of reading and discussing the work itself. "The meetings give us a chance to interact socially with teachers from the other departments and with the principal and assistant principal who are also in the group," she observed. "The program helps us recognize that even adults prefer different genres, so kids also need to be allowed to choose. It's interesting because people say, 'I'm really not a fiction reader—I like autobiographies or I like historical novels.' Sometimes we don't give our kids the chance to say that."

Reinforcing Reading

In keeping with their comprehensive approach to reading, Capuano, Nolan, and other Harshman faculty recognize that reading must also be valued and reinforced at home. Parents Sharing Books is another Lilly-sponsored reading initiative designed to give parents and children some "quality time" together. Each month, participating parents and children are asked to select a book, read it, and then come to school to discuss it. The meetings offer parents a chance to learn how to discuss books, build rapport with their children, and socialize.

Twice a year Harshman holds a special reading week, when parents, celebrities, and members of the community are invited to the school to read aloud to students. Guest readers include local businesspeople, newscasters, radio and television personalities, athletes, political leaders, and the like. Each week usually has a theme, such as "Hats Off to Reading" or "Sock It to Reading." As many as sixty individuals volunteer each year. Readers choose their own material. Nolan coordinates the program, sending out scores of invitations to community leaders annually. "I read, the custodian reads, everybody reads," she said. "The focus is on making sure the kids aren't disappointed."

Guest readers like community activist Dennis West love the opportunity to read to the students. West picks his material carefully, making sure that it will hold the students' attention. One year he chose a book about voodoo. "My wife had been in the Peace Corps in Togo," he explained. "The book was set there, and I wanted to make that connection. We live one block from Harshman, and I wanted the students to know that there are people who have had these experiences in their midst."

Another year, West chose a story about the first woman chief of the Cherokee Tribe who worked hard to promote self-employment for her people. While the Guest Reader program is designed to motivate students to read, it also helps with public relations. "Most students are very attentive and well mannered," said West. "It seems like a pretty friendly school—kids are connected with the faculty."

Reading Across the Curriculum

Capuano and her staff know that, to integrate reading into the core curriculum, teachers in all disciplines need training and ongoing support. Language arts teachers also need new strategies to enhance their efforts. Therefore, Harshman initiated a pilot teacher exchange program, drawing teachers from the IPS Education Center, the district's own staff development office. Once again, funding came from the Lilly Endowment.

Exchange teachers are regular classroom teachers who have been released from their normal duties for a full year. Each receives training in effective teaching and learning, as well as peer coaching and peer collaboration. The exchange teachers worked one-on-one with the Harshman faculty to improve students' reading skills and teachers' teaching skills.

To introduce the program, Mary Lynn Woods, the exchange program's coordinator, presented a day-long workshop in the fall of 1991, demonstrating reading and writing strategies. Afterward approximately twenty Harshman teachers from several disciplines volunteered to be paired with an exchange teacher. The exchange teachers visited their partners' classrooms three times that year, spending a total of six hours with their colleagues.

During their first visit, the exchange teachers demonstrated some of the workshop ideas in the classroom. On their return, they worked with their partners to design and teach a lesson embodying those ideas. During their third and final visit of the year, the exchange teachers observed their partners teach a lesson modeled on the previous sessions. After their classroom observations, the exchange teachers met briefly with their partners to discuss what they had observed.

A Classroom Visit

During the first year of the pilot program, Woods was the exchange teacher for Claudia Evans, a seventh-grade language arts teacher. Evans is one of several talented teachers on the Hope House team, as well as the chair of the Harshman language arts department. Evans has a great deal of faith in her students' abilities, and they live up to her expectations. "She believes that kids can read and write, that they have the ability to think abstractly and develop symbolic language," said Woods. "When you treat students that way, then they're going to respond."

On May 19, 1992, Woods visited Evans's seventh-grade language arts class. Woods and Evans had been partners since the beginning of the school year, and this was their final meeting before summer vacation. An intense woman, Evans seems at first glance a bit cold and difficult to approach. Yet on this morning, many of the students came over to hug and kiss her as they arrived in the classroom.

The lesson on this particular day was about symbolism. Evans had arranged a variety of objects on a table at the center of the room: a pair of salt and pepper shakers, a sneaker, a rock, a plastic puzzle cube, a candle. She began by talking about symbols and how a single object can represent or suggest a series of seemingly unrelated ideas. This discussion of symbolism was clearly not new to the class. The students seemed to pick up on it quickly. Evans asked what kinds of ideas might be symbolized by the salt and pepper shakers, which were white and brown, respectively. "Racism" was one of the instant replies. When she asked for ideas about the rock, the students came up with "strength," "foundation," and "nature" as possible answers.

Evans went on to talk about how, starting with a series of symbolic associations, they could develop their ideas into a piece of writing. Using the single sneaker as a starting point, she read aloud this poem by Carlos Moore, a student in the class:

> The shoe that has the blues was red as fire
> It was bought in a store on a day it rained
> It was smelly and stinky, but who was to blame?
> It's gotta hole in its front and striped lines on its side
> . . . and
> When others buy shoes, they just pass it by . . .
> All of its life it has wanted to be on somebody's feet
> It wanted to be owned, all day until night when
> the hard winds blow
> It will always be around because
> belonging is only a dream . . .
> Life will never be real
> For this shoe with the blues.

Carlos was obviously well-known to the other students. (He was repeatedly in trouble, we later found out, in most of his classes, except for Evans's.) The students were impressed: "Carlos wrote that? That's good."

After a little more discussion, the students began working individually on the assignment. Many of them drew pictures or "webs" of the images they had come up with, while others moved on to composing their verses. No one seemed to have trouble understanding the purpose of the assignment. They had all grasped the concept of symbolism and its relationship to writing.

Lessons like these result in student writing of very high quality. Here are some examples drawn from three different collections of "Harshman Verses":

A candle is a lovely thing
It makes no noise at all
But softly gives itself away
While quite unselfishly
It grows small.

Jason Stewart

White candle
In the resisting dark:
Midnight

Des Ire

The Rock (A Look Inside)

I lay along, underground
I don't have friends
What have I done . . . Wrong?
When can I leave?
I don't have feet to walk around
That's why I am picked up and
Thrown back to the ground
Only if I had a face to show you what's Inside
To show I am Something . . .

A Somebody
While I'm still on this Earth I have a beautiful
Inside Face.

Semorris Moore

Puzzle Pieces

My life is like a puzzle piece
I think I have it all together . . . Then,
I'm missing a piece.
I try to find it
But there's no use.
It's fallen on the ground somewhere
and I can't seem to put it out of my mind.

Samantha Winks

Winter

Frogs burrow into the mud
Snails alone by themselves
As I air my guilts
Preparing for the cold.
Dogs grow more hair
Mothers make oatmeal
And little boys and girls sip
Father-Johns Old Fashioned Cough Syrup.
Bears store fat
As chipmunks gather nuts and
I Collect Books
For the coming winter.

Monyana Mills

Evans's work does not end with helping students develop verbal pictures or enhancing their ability to create symbols, analogies, and metaphors. She helps students confront their feelings by talking with them about her own childhood, which was not easy. She also shares her own writing, drawing on her experiences in college. "The teachers always wrote with the class," she said, "and I always observed them as they were writing. They seemed to be having so much fun doing it. I thought, Gee, they must take this seriously. My kids do the same thing. When I comment, they comment on papers, and when I write notes, they write back and forth to each other."

After the classroom observation, Woods met privately with Evans to discuss what she had observed. She praised the well-crafted lesson and offered additional insights about how it might be further improved. Then, Evans, Woods, Capuano, and the other exchange teachers and their partners met in the library to debrief on the year's program and plan for the coming year. The consensus was that the exchange teachers needed to spend more time in their partners' classrooms at the beginning of the year to develop a deeper sense of trust. The exchange teachers agreed to come for three days in the fall and return later in the year after their partners had had a chance to practice their new teaching strategies.

Community Involvement

When Capuano came to Harshman, she knew that it was essential to involve the community in promoting change. Furthermore, she recognized that the community had strengths that she could draw on: a sense of pride, a history of strong civic leaders, a number of community-based organizations and agencies, and positive social networks. "I'm a firm believer that you can't do it all in your building," she said.

Capuano's efforts to reach out to the community were well received by community members who were just as willing to reach in. Before Capuano became principal, a small group of concerned residents had already joined to form Community Council 101, a parent-teacher planning group. The council has several goals: to give Harshman students a sense of belonging during their stay at the school, give local business and industry a chance to see the good side of the school, and bring all the neighborhood resources to bear in addressing the school's needs. The council includes Capuano, a few teachers in the school, three or four local businesspeople, and three or four parents who are community residents.

According to Marty Miles, a member of the Near East Side Community Organization that helped create the 101 council, the community has always been concerned about the school, but its problems had seemed daunting. "Now there's a sense of hope that was not there two or three years ago," she said.

The 101 council arranges parent workshops, though it learned early on that parent participation depended on finding nonthreatening things for them to do. Computer classes have been especially successful. Since most adults do not know how to use computers, no one is at a disadvantage. The classes give participants a chance to play with mathematics and language arts software and learn informally, without having to admit that they need help.

Once parents began to see the school as a friendly place, they asked for additional education programs. At the parents' request, Capuano started a GED (Graduate Equivalency Diploma) class at the school, held on Monday and Wednesday evenings. The council also helped create the Parents Sharing Books program, and it sponsored a recognition evening for honor roll students and their parents. Parents now have their own room in the school building where they are free to drop in and talk with one another, coordinate volunteer efforts, and discuss school concerns.

The PALS Program

Harshman also has a buddy system, similar to the big brother and big sister concept, that helps link the school with key members of the community. Called PALS (Positive Achievement Leads to Success), it was an outgrowth of the Stanley K. Lacey leadership development program. Each year, this program runs a series of seminars and workshops for community and business leaders in Indianapolis, one of which is devoted entirely to education. In 1991, Capuano invited the group to visit Harshman for the day. The group was so captivated by the faculty's vision for the school that it devised the PALS program as a way of staying involved.

PALS brings together a community person, two students (a high-achieving student and a student who is not achieving up to capacity), and a teacher. During the 1991–92 school year, approximately forty-two community people and forty-two teachers served as PALS to eighty-four Harshman students. Everyone in the program had to sign a contract—students, teachers, and community members alike. Under the terms of the contract, teachers are required to contact the community person and invite him or her to school once every two weeks. Both adults are supposed to contact the students' parents once a month, by phone or letter. The teachers are asked to contact their PALS once a week, while the community members meet with them at least biweekly.

To prepare community volunteers, Harshman held an in-service program, explaining the needs and characteristics of middle school children. "I told them, 'This is what a middle school child is like,'" recalled Assistant Principal DyLynn Phelps. "I listed their characteristics—high and low, happy and sad. Then, everyone paired off and exchanged phone numbers and interests. Since then, they've gone all kinds of places."

Phelps was a PAL to two seventh graders: Monica and Tajah. Debbie Blackwell, who handles public relations for the city of Indianapolis, was their community PAL. When asked what Blackwell had done with them, both girls chimed in excitedly, finishing each other's sentences. They described trips to the zoo, Blackwell's office, the theater, a bookstore, the children's museum.

"What do you see as the benefits of the PALS program?" we asked. Both girls replied, "It's mostly just fun." Monica added, "Well, we do talk about serious issues and stuff." Twice a week, teachers hold after-school sessions for PALS students. "We go in there and sit down, and we just talk about almost anything," said Monica. "Like our problems," continued Tajah. "They help us solve them."

Planting Roots in the Community

Harshman Middle School and the community are also building bridges through a number of gardening projects. The Just Say Grow project was the brainchild of a community resident who wanted to celebrate Earth Day. Eastside Community Investments, Inc., a nonprofit community development corporation, has taken the idea and built an annual celebration around it. The project involves planting trees and shrubs to beautify the neighborhood.

Harshman students are part of this community effort. Students and residents work side by side to plant flowers, shrubs, and twelve-foot trees along 10th Street in front of the school.

Dennis West views this as one way to motivate students to take greater pride and interest in their community. "Unfortunately, I think a lot of kids who come through this neighborhood believe that making it means leaving here," he commented. "Hopefully, we are beginning to create a new way of thinking about our community which says, 'You can make it, and you can make it here.'"

Marty Miles helped coordinate student participation in the Just Say Grow tree-planting effort, working closely with the Guardian Vikings, a student leadership group. Miles is convinced that the program helps link the school and the community. "When you're with a team of kids planting a tree, wheeling the mulch down the street, you get to talk with them," she said. "They themselves were saying this was neat, and the community, this neighborhood, really needed that."

Taking the Just Say Grow concept one step further, two innovative science and mathematics teachers, Donna Chastang and Linda Gagyi, joined forces to create a vegetable garden in the school's courtyard. They designed the project to combine experiential learning, interdisciplinary instruction, and community service. "We went to a grant-writing seminar at GTE," said Gagyi. "We just decided to go for it. We assumed that our first year's grant would get rejected, and we would just polish it up for the next year." To their surprise, the teachers received $7,000 from GTE to run the actual project and another $2,500 each for professional development. "We must have done something right," admitted Gagyi.

The project began in the winter with the students conducting germination studies that linked math, science, and gardening skills. "We had the kids fold up the seeds in wet paper and check them every day," explained Chastang. "We did comparisons and graphed which seeds germinated most quickly. We computed percentages and averages and things like that." Gagyi added, "We brought in social studies, growth rate comparisons, and weather studies. We got a lot of weather equipment for each house to have. Hopefully, they will continue those measurements year to year—comparing last year's weather to this year's."

According to Chastang, the garden is especially important because it gives the youngsters a chance to get out of their seats and outside the building. They have an opportunity to do physical work while learning science and mathematics. "It also gives them a chance to work on something that they can actually see transform before their very eyes," said Chastang. "The first time that the lettuce started to sprout, they were saying, 'Oh! The lettuce is up!' And so it gives them a hands-on feeling that they can actually see something that's been accomplished."

Come harvest time, Chastang's students are given first crack at picking the vegetables: lettuce, tomatoes, cucumbers, and so on. Whatever produce remains unclaimed is given to the homeless shelters in the neighborhood. Thus the garden gives Harshman yet another mechanism for contributing to the welfare of the local community.

Moving into the Light

Today, Harshman Middle School can be described, both literally and figuratively, as having moved from darkness to light. Not long ago, the school had inadequate lighting; the hallways were dark and bare. Today the school has new lighting, and hallway walls are decorated with student poetry, pictures, reports, and other work. Large numbers of students are using the school's on-site health clinic, students are reading more than ever before, and their poems are published in the school's collections of verses. Community volunteers make frequent classroom visits, and the trees the students planted flourish on the street outside.

Change is beginning to show up in hard data. For example, attendance at Harshman rose steadily from 79 percent in 1990–91 to 90.5 percent in 1992–93. And students' scores on standardized tests of achievement have also shown modest signs of improvement in both reading and mathematics.

Reflecting on these changes, community activist Marty Miles said, "In the late eighties, when my children were junior high age, I was pleased that they did not have to attend school here. They were able to go to the magnet junior high, which was someplace else. The image of Harshman at that time was very poor, in terms of both academic performance and atmosphere. Just three or four years ago, there was nothing on the walls—nothing! It was dark, and the mood in the building was not exciting or fun. It was depressing. I have seen tremendous change just in the last two years. In little things—the mood of the teachers that I've had a chance to talk to and the sense of excitement about learning."

Hardly a miracle, the Harshman success story is the result of hard work and commitment. Assistant Principal Phelps would add that teamwork has been key in turning the school around. "Everyone was trying to do a good job before Marcia [Capuano] came," she said, "but everyone was in their own little corner trying to do it by themselves. Her focus has been: we have to work as a team.

We've tried to change the mindset of staff members from 'me, me, me' to 'we, we, we.'"

Capuano's energy and enthusiasm make her an ideal team leader. As Claudia Evans explained, "When I see somebody as strong as she is, we, the teachers, want to work harder, work together more." Capuano was one of four persons nationally to receive the 1993 Petra Foundation Award, which recognizes unsung heros working to promote racial equality and social justice. Surprised and somewhat embarrassed by the award, she exclaimed, "But it doesn't seem right. This award shouldn't be given to me—I don't deserve it. It should be given to the whole faculty."

Also responsible for change at Harshman is the positive "can do" philosophy of the staff. According to Phelps, there used to be a tendency at Harshman to blame the children and their families for their problems. "If the child was not achieving, teachers said it was because of the home. We've tried to refocus that," explained Phelps. "The effective schools literature says it shouldn't matter where the child comes from. We have to do what we need to here in school in order to help that child achieve."

Capuano's practical and entrepreneurial approach to problems is yet another reason for the school's success. Like other principals in large urban school systems, she has used whatever resources are at hand, sometimes going outside the system if necessary in order to create change. "Marcia operates from the questions What's the problem? What's needed to begin to deal with it? And where can I find it?" said Miles. "She just doesn't let what other people think or anything else stand in her way."

Capuano credits MGIP with helping bring about change. "The Middle Grades Assessment Program provided a structure and a support base for action," she said. "It helped outline what was needed." MGIP also provided additional resources for Harshman staff to visit other schools and communities outside of Indianapolis. "There's no way that my teachers could go to Delaware to see middle schools that have been transformed," she said. "So you rely on grants like MGIP for that." Both Capuano and her staff have participated in a number of MGIP Network–sponsored activities aimed at promoting teaming and interdisciplinary instruction. In addition, several Harshman teachers have applied for and received teacher incentive (MGIP-X) grants through which they have designed their own theme-based interdisciplinary curriculum units.

Most important, MGIP provided overall direction. When Capuano wanted to eliminate corporal punishment, MGIP "provided a structure and a support base," she said. "Because of MGIP, you don't have to fight for what you believe in," she added. "Teachers and administrators are supported—we have a common language." In Capuano's view, the most important feature of MGIP is its central concern for adolescents and middle school issues. "It provides a guiding light and a focus, the ability to make things happen, and people that want to make them happen," she asserted.

One of those people is MGIP consultant Len Finkelstein. He has been a consultant to IPS since the beginning of the MGIP program. A former teacher, principal, district superintendent, and superintendent, Finkelstein ascribes much of his success as a consultant to his ongoing availability for almost seven years. "They were used to the 'program of the month' consultant," he told us, "and had grown heavy, protective armor for purposes of self-preservation." Finkelstein served as a self-styled father confessor, cheerleader, facilitator, mirror, and constructive critic. After a few years, an astounding level of trust and comfort developed.

Roberta Bowers, the former MGIP coordinator for IPS, noted that, as an outsider, Finkelstein could see things objectively and say things that needed to be said. "We need that external prodding," she said. "In an educational bureaucracy, it's important to ruffle feathers sometimes." Bowers herself arranged for staff development, made regular visits to monitor progress, and provided Harshman with information and assistance on request.

In the fall of 1993, IPS reorganized its schools, moving sixth graders in with seventh and eighth graders. Capuano feels that

MGIP was instrumental in helping IPS move to the middle school concept. "People had the potential and had really worked toward it," she said, "but they weren't able to accomplish it before."

As a result of this grade-level reorganization and other districtwide changes, Harshman no longer serves the same population it did when we first visited. It has become a magnet school with a heavy emphasis on science, mathematics, and technology, and it now attracts students from all over the school system. According to Capuano, many new parents have proclaimed Harshman "the best-kept secret in the district." Most had expected lots of graffiti and were pleasantly surprised by the school's aesthetics, the wealth of technology, the teachers' caring attitude, and the wide variety of exemplary projects. "Even the district sees us in a different light," Capuano reported. "We were recently chosen to host a major kick-off for the mayor."

As impressive as the past few years have been, Capuano and her staff consider the job at Harshman far from finished. "The mountain is still ahead, high and steep," she said. "We have come up the mountain—we are not at the base anymore. But there is still a long way to go." One continuing challenge is ensuring that all classrooms foster active, inquiry-based learning. Another is finding alternative ways to assess students' progress, to capture the many ways in which they are learning to think, solve problems, and communicate. Capuano would also like to see alternative programs developed for those students who, even with support services, have a hard time making it in the regular school setting.

Sometimes Capuano gets impatient with the slow pace of change. "There is too much to do in too little time," she lamented. "Education is a gift—it's the only thing that will pull children out of poverty. The time for change is now. Every passing day or year means more kids whom the system fails."

Chapter Four

A Team That Works

> Good teachers are not afraid to laugh or cry, to be
> honest, to have integrity, to share their personal
> lives.
>
> *—Ernest Boyer*

Decatur Middle School sits in the center of a modest residential
neighborhood in the heart of Decatur Township on the southwest
edge of Indianapolis. It is considered a pioneer in the middle school
reform effort in Indiana. Asked to nominate outstanding schools
for us to visit in researching this book, several MGIP staff members
and consultants placed Decatur at the top of their lists. Teachers
and administrators from across the state have visited the school to
learn more about teaming, interdisciplinary instruction, advisory
programs, and other aspects of middle school reform.

Decatur has also won school incentive awards, based on demonstrated improvements in students' academic performance, each
year they have been offered by the state of Indiana. From 1987 to
1991, the number of low-income youngsters attending the school
increased from 25 to 29 percent. During this same period, reading
scores increased from a median of 48.8 to 54.6, and mathematics
scores also increased slightly.

In this chapter we present a close-up of one outstanding set of
teachers who helped pioneer teaming at Decatur Middle School.
It is a picture of teaming at its best, a portrait of the possible. These
teachers showed us that teaming is at the heart of personalizing
middle schools. They learn from and support one another; they
respect their students and set high expectations for them. To help
their students cope with the normal concerns and fears of early adolescence, they are willing to share their own life experiences and

inner feelings. And, working together, they create rich, interdisciplinary curriculum units that address not only significant social issues but also young adolescents' interests and concerns.

Decatur's Team 8C illustrates a fundamental tenet of middle-level education. You cannot separate social and emotional development from intellectual development or affective education from academic achievement; they are inextricably intertwined. At the same time, highly successful teams like this one raise critical questions for middle-grades reformers. How can middle schools ensure that all teams in the building work smoothly and effectively? And how can they ensure that those who are on the cutting edge—the early pioneers—help blaze the trail for others?

Jackson and Jewel

Jackson Fox was on a path familiar to many young American black males: failing grades, dropping out, drugs, and alienation. An obviously intelligent, proud, articulate, and handsome eighth grader at Decatur Middle School, Jackson told us about his life and its turning points.

"My neighborhood has a lot of violence," he said. "I had a cousin who sold drugs. He bought me things. I always thought, well, I can go out and be like him. And I thought, doing bad in school—it ain't gonna hurt nobody but me. I thought I could sell drugs like my cousin. Then one day, my mother told me my cousin passed away. That hurt me. This was my world. He was everything to me, and he had passed away. And then I didn't want to hear about schooling, or how to read, or grammar."

The teachers at Decatur Middle School are organized into interdisciplinary teams, with each team responsible for about 150 students. The existence of this team structure, and of one team in particular, were crucial factors in the story of what happened to Jackson next.

"I can't even remember what team I was on in seventh grade," he told us, "but I had a real rough time with them. I made some mistakes, and I got kicked out of school. My grades were extremely bad. This year I tried to make it better, but I got in trouble again and I was on the verge of getting suspended. I just wasn't getting along with some of my teachers."

The trouble was provoked partly by Jackson's emerging sense of himself as an African American in a predominantly white school and his exposure to black culture and politics. He had started to participate in a neighborhood youth program at Indianapolis's Broadway United Methodist Church and to read about Malcolm X. Malcolm became Jackson's hero. His new awareness of racial struggle brought him into conflict with white teachers and students at Decatur. Twelve percent of the students at the school are black—virtually all of them bused there from the inner-city neighborhood of Mapleton–Fall Creek as a result of a desegregation order dating back to the early 1980s.

Leroy Blocher is the wrestling coach at Decatur and the science teacher on Team 8C. He knew Jackson through wrestling and recognized that the young man was in trouble. "He was on one of the other eighth-grade teams," Blocher told us. "His science class was right across the hall from mine, and I noticed a lot of the time he was pushing, shoving, not doing well. I talked to his science teacher, who said he was having trouble with him all the time. Most of his problems came from the Malcolm X thing. He was preaching about Malcolm X in the hallway and about black-white conflict. So I had a talk with him one day about it. I think he liked the idea that I showed some concern for him. And at the semester break, I asked if we could take him on our team and give him a new beginning."

"Mr. Blocher asked me if I wanted to be on 8C," Jackson recalled. "'It'll help you a lot,' he said. 'We'll work with you.' I said, 'I don't care because I'm having a hard time now.' So they arranged it, and second semester I was on their team. They gave me a new beginning. They told me that all the things in my past was over. Just concentrate on the future. 'You're in a new family,' they said."

For Jackson, life on Team 8C changed everything. "It's the difference between night and day," said Blocher. "His whole attitude toward school changed. Before, he saw everything in terms of race. If a teacher had a confrontation with him, he saw that as a white teacher talking to a black student." Blocher, on the other hand, saw the critical issues as ones of value, love, and respect. "We give some value to Jackson's ideas," he said. "We don't treat him like a dumb kid who has no value. We just love him to death."

Jackson himself described the transformation this way: "I was pulling Cs and Ds first semester, and now I'm up to Bs and Cs. I'm doing a good job. I think 8C is a great team. More teachers should help their kids more and not be so strict at times. Give them a chance to grow.

"If I don't understand something, I get frustrated. I get frustrated real quick. On my old team, it was all work. They would just give you lessons. They'd show you how to do it two times and then you'd miss. Team 8C is not like that, because they work with you and show you, and they make learning fun. I think you have to have that, because some kids get lost. They'll work with you during lunch periods. Any time you need them, you just come and talk to them and they'll help you out.

"This semester has taught me how to get along with people," Jackson said. "It showed me that you could get along with teachers. I used to have a hard time with teachers. They didn't like me, so I didn't like them. I used to see how far I could push them. If I get frustrated in high school, I know I can always come back to these teachers. They say, 'We'll always be here for you,' and I know they will. I'll never forget them."

Jewel Murphy's story, like Jackson's, is not unusual in 1990s America. A beautiful eighth grader, with long blond hair and maturity beyond her years, she had recently reached the point of emotional breakdown as the result of severe family dysfunction. What is unusual, perhaps, is Jewel's ability to describe the sources of stress in her life and talk about the roles her teachers—Team 8C—have played in helping her survive.

"My mother is hardly ever around," Jewel said when we asked about her home life. "She's on disability, but she goes out to bars. My mother's an alcoholic, and it's hard to live with an alcoholic. My dad—I've been scared of him my entire life, and I can't talk to him. So most of the time I'm alone at home, and I have to take care of myself. I do the laundry and keep up the house. The only thing I'm not doing is paying the bills. As a matter of fact, I can't even remember my childhood. I can't remember growing up and playing with any of the kids. Only that when I was little I was picked on a lot by the other kids."

Jewel described for us the approach that Team 8C uses to keep kids from fighting: "Some of us do fight now and then, because we're mad at somebody and we just don't know how to get back at them. The teachers try to keep us out of fights. Their way of doing that is talking to us. If you've got a problem with somebody, they want you to come straight to them. That way you don't have to be seen down at the office all the time. And you don't feel you have to beat some kid up, or he won't leave you alone.

"When some other adults tell you that you have to make decisions for yourself, you're always thinking about the bad because of the way they say it. These teachers tell it to us in a different way. They say, 'You could do good—you're not always bad. There's nothing terrible about you.' That's the reason why Ms. Stahlhut has that big poster on her wall that says, 'Make change, succeed.' That's what they want us to do: succeed in life.

"So now, when there's a fight, the teachers will come up and say, 'You can't do this. Why are you hurting them?' And we'll go back and apologize. Most of us get along really well. We don't give each other dirty looks, and if we don't have anything nice to say to each other, we just don't say nothing at all."

Jewel described the powerful bond that developed between students and teachers as a result of this willingness to intervene, to get involved. "Some of the students would rather live at school than go home," she said, and clearly she included herself in that group. "I just got out of the hospital, out of an adolescent unit, and my teachers were totally behind me. They talked to me a lot. They helped me any way they could so that I could go on with my schooling.

"All year I've had straight As and Bs, and maybe one C, and that was with their help, their counseling, their care," said Jewel. "Because at home I didn't get much of that at all. I hope that when I get into high school I'll find some people just like 'em. I don't know how I'm going to react to leaving when this school year's out. It went by so fast. I wouldn't switch 'em for the world. I wouldn't go to any other team. Never."

"A Little Bit of Everyone"

Some of the townships that surround Indianapolis are wealthy, homogeneous bedroom communities. Not Decatur Township. "We have a little bit of everyone here," Principal Wally Bourke told us. "Nearly seven out of eight students live within the township itself. We have a very large population that comes from a formerly industrial area called Mars Hill. The industries have all died and gone away and left a low-income white population there."

Other students come from the lower- and middle-class suburban housing developments that checker the area. Still others come from little villages dating back to the 1800s, and a few come from the rather extensive outlying agricultural areas of the township. Twelve percent of the students, as noted earlier, are bused to Decatur from the virtually all-black Mapleton–Fall Creek neighborhood, thirty blocks on the other side of downtown Indianapolis.

Until the fall of 1991, Decatur Middle School served only eight hundred students in grades seven and eight. That year, a new addition to the building allowed the township's sixth graders, who had moved to the elementary schools several years before, to rejoin the middle school. Now Decatur is really two schools in one, serving about 1,260 sixth, seventh, and eighth graders.

The new building, housing the seventh and eighth grades, was designed specifically to accommodate interdisciplinary teams. Teachers on a given team have adjoining classrooms, stretching along a wide, well-lit hallway. In close proximity to each team's classrooms is a large, comfortable team meeting space, equipped with a computer and telephone.

Teaming: The Centerpiece of Change

"The centerpiece of what has happened here has been the creation of teacher teams," said Bourke. "It's been the vehicle through which we've done a lot of other things." A key reason that Decatur Middle School instituted interdisciplinary teaming was to help deal with its wide range of students, each with differing abilities and needs. Each team serves a diverse group of youngsters—Decatur was one of the first middle schools in the state to eliminate tracking students by achievement level.

"Teaming is critical in meeting the needs of young adolescents," explained Marilyn Bunner, chair of the social studies department and a member of the school's Middle Grades Improvement Program Planning Committee. "Some of us felt that children got lost when they came to middle school because they had no real identity. They had a lot of different teachers, going to different classrooms. We saw teaming as a way, first, of having a kid belong. It also gives us an opportunity to follow these children more closely in terms of their academics and their social development."

Teaming is the first line of defense for students' problems, but teachers are not alone in their efforts. Decatur Middle School also has a strong student assistance program offering guidance, counseling, and support services to children and their families. At its core are preventive meetings—involving team members, assistant principals, and counselors—where participants discuss individual students as well as general problems facing the school. In addition, students receive needed support through peer tutors, high school mentors, and after-school discussion groups. And the school's at-risk counselor runs more than a dozen peer support groups dealing with problems such as substance-abusing parents, divorce, child molestation, pregnancy, and violence.

In seventh and eighth grade, each interdisciplinary team includes five teachers—two language arts, one science, one mathematics, and one social studies—with a common group of about 150 students. Learning disabilities teachers and their students are also assigned to the teams. In sixth grade, because there is only one language arts teacher for each group of 150 students, there are only four teachers to a team.

Daily team planning time is considered essential. Seventh- and eighth-grade team members have both an individual preparation period and a team preparation period every day. Laughing, Bourke said it took him four years to work all the kinks out of the seventh- and eighth-grade schedules. "The wonderful Dr. Swensson left without finishing his dream of a team schedule," he said, referring to his respected predecessor and mentor. "I was supposed to develop this schedule for the following school year, and it kept me up at night. As a matter of fact, the pattern for meeting all of the interests in this schedule came to me in the middle of the night. I literally sat up and wrote this stuff down."

After that first year, Bourke experimented with alternatives, and he was still not satisfied when we visited. "The one thing it does not do well," he said, "is provide teachers with flexible blocks of time." One reason was the team design: each included two language arts teachers. Eventually, Bourke found a way to take advantage of this situation: he created an extended language arts block that placed two forty-minute periods back to back.

Many of the language arts teachers chose to divide their students into two groups, with each taking half and teaching three eighty-minute language arts blocks a day. Bourke pointed out that these teachers "coordinate all of their instruction so that spelling, reading, and writing are integrated in some form. Spelling words are extracted from what they read in literature and used in what they write, and what they write is related to what they read."

Team 8C chose not to use the extended language arts block in this manner. "They didn't like it," Bourke told us, "because they become so attached to their kids. They couldn't stand not having any contact with half the kids on the team. So they switch them. They still coordinate the whole language approach, however."

A Portrait of a Team That Works

The stories of Jackson Fox and Jewel Murphy are hardly unique at Decatur Middle School or other urban and suburban schools across the country. Team 8C has developed a reputation for taking in young adolescents with differing needs and abilities, including those who are at risk of failure, and giving them a new beginning.

At the same time, Jackson's story in particular confirms what other researchers and observers have already pointed out: that the mere existence of an interdisciplinary team structure does not in itself create a positive environment in which all kids can thrive. Jackson's seventh-grade team and the first eighth-grade team to which he was assigned both failed to reach him.

What makes Team 8C work? How do its members manage to attend to the needs of approximately 150 students and still reach out to other troubled youngsters, like Jackson, who are not even on their team? To begin with, the five members of Team 8C— Bruce Simon, Dee Stahlhut, Pam Gambill, Leroy Blocher, and Jim Crane—share an abiding love of young adolescents, a commitment to their success, a willingness to experiment, and a profound respect for each other. (Since our visit, Gambill has left to become a media center specialist at Carl G. Fisher School #1 in Speedway, Indiana. Amy Hurlburt, an Eastern Kentucky University graduate, replaced

Gambill in the 1992–93 school year and, according to her colleagues, "has been a wonderful asset to the team.")

A mock "help wanted" ad prepared by the team offers a telling glimpse of its approach to teaching:

WANTED: TEAM TEACHERS
Only Caring, Loving Risk Takers Need Apply.

Caring, sharing personal experiences, rewarding, praising, encouraging, setting limits are all ingredients of this team that works. By their own behavior—fighting, laughing, hugging, disagreeing—they model what it means to be a family, to love and respect one another despite individual differences. They also believe strongly in the importance of making connections with their students both emotionally and physically, with a pat on the back, a touch on the shoulder, or a ruffling of hair. Yet, they never lose sight of their ultimate objective: helping youngsters learn.

The Members of the Team

Bruce Simon, 8C's social studies teacher, has more than twenty years of experience in the classroom. It is easy to recognize him in the Decatur lunchroom: he is the one walking up and down ruffling the boys' crew cuts. When Jackson Fox walks by in the hallway, Simon calls out, with obvious affection, "There goes the Fox," eliciting a shy smile from the youth. This teacher seems always to be making connections.

Simon's classroom would probably shock a lot of traditional junior high school teachers. He lets students sit wherever they want—even turning their backs on him if they feel like it. As students work individually or in small groups, he walks around the room casually looking in on each one, having brief conversations, patting a shoulder. He rarely raises his voice, preferring to use gentle irony to control student behavior. When one girl persists in talking to her friend rather than focusing on the task at hand, Simon calls out from across the room, "Shantee, you'll have to be noisier. I keep missing what you're saying."

Simon does not much like history textbooks. His approach to teaching about World War I, for example, offers a stark contrast to the typical textbook lessons emphasizing dates and names of battles and generals. Instead, Simon teaches about life at the front— what it meant to be a soldier in the trenches. His students do learn facts: that World War I was the first time in history that armies fought from stable positions, for example. But Simon is not content to just lecture. His classes first watch the classic film *All Quiet on the Western Front*. Then they go out on the school grounds to dig their own trenches with shovels and picks. The students' trenches do not reach the six- to eight-foot depth of actual World War I trenches, of course; they rarely get beyond a few inches. But they learn, in a way that no textbook or lecture could duplicate, the sheer magnitude of the task, how muddy the trenches were, how hard it was to shore them up in the rain, and how filled they were with slugs and other crawling things.

When it comes to assessing what students have learned, Simon asks them to evaluate their own and others' work on the trenches using questions like these: "Whom did you work with on the trench?" "What grade do you deserve on your trench?" "Who helped/didn't help you?" "What did they do?" "What grade do they deserve?" "What about the trench was different than you expected?"

We sat in on one of Simon's World War I classes. The students had been reading primary sources, including first-hand accounts by soldiers. In class he painted a horrific portrait of life in the trenches: how it must have felt to crawl and burrow in the mud, the lack of food, and the ubiquitous rats, which the German soldiers often wound up shooting and eating when their rations ran out.

Through his vivid description, life at the front became all too real. Lice infested the soldiers' clothes, chewed their flesh, and had to be burned off. Shrapnel blew off arms and legs, and frightened young soldiers stumbled over dead bodies, discovering stray heads and limbs. Many soldiers suffered from trenchfoot after standing in cold water for long periods. Some young soldiers were literally scared to death. "Shell-shocked," they heedlessly ran directly into the line of enemy fire.

Simon contrasted these images with the sanitized, glorified vision of war in many contemporary films like *Rambo*. Some students groaned at the grim details, but all sat spellbound. It was clear from their questions, which Simon answered thoughtfully and honestly, that they would not easily forget this lesson about the horrors of warfare.

It is also clear that every element of Simon's teaching—his classroom management techniques, his interactions with individual students, his analysis of what is important in the material to be covered, his relating the lesson to the students' own experience, and his way of evaluating their work—grows directly from a profound love and respect for young people and a deep commitment to his subject. Simon's students return this love and respect and respond to his enthusiasm for history in equal measure.

Dee Stahlhut, one of two language arts teachers on Team 8C, is talking with a group of 8C girls at lunch. She is twenty-five but looks much younger. In her T-shirt and slacks, she might easily be mistaken for one of her students. She flits from student to student in the group, hugging, touching, whispering, encouraging, prodding as she moves about.

Stahlhut is the spark plug of the team—the cheerleader, social worker, and guardian angel. Her passion is getting students to express themselves through writing. As Jewel told us, "Ms. Stahlhut has us take out our frustrations and our happiness on paper—in poetry, in reports, in anything."

When we walk into her classroom, we find her students busy creating their own original storybooks for the second graders at the nearby Valley Mills Elementary School. Six students are sprawled on the floor writing. Others are seated at five large tables, working in groups of two to four students. Despite the informal atmosphere, the activity in the room seems highly focused. Pens are busily scratching, and there is a constant quiet buzz, punctuated by occasional bursts of laughter. Stahlhut works alongside her students. She, too, is preparing a book, which she plans to present to her young nephew Justin.

The students began this extended project by reading some second-grade-level stories and thinking about what they had in common. Then each student interviewed a second grader at the elementary school to learn about his or her background and interests. The child's answers, recorded in the author's Valley Mills portfolio, help provide ideas for the kind of story that is likely to appeal to the second grader. Other things will eventually find their way into each student's portfolio: a brief narrative entitled "About the Author," a picture of the author, and a story map that provides an overview of the characters and events in the story. As students complete their drafts and make revisions, these too will become part of the portfolio.

Today most of the students are composing their first drafts, which are due next week. Stahlhut tells us that four or five of the boys in the class are having trouble getting started. She needs to give them some extra help, but their study hall time does not coincide with hers. This could pose a problem for some teachers, but Stahlhut is undaunted. She has invited the boys to meet her after school three days next week, over pizza or ice cream, to brainstorm ideas, develop story maps, and start writing. No one on her team is allowed to fail.

Once the stories have been drafted, Stahlhut and the other students will critique them. Then students will spend up to three days in the computer lab making revisions. Knowing that their books will be published helps motivate the students to make them perfect. Once the text is in final draft, students will prepare a publishable manuscript complete with illustrations. Finally, the class will visit the Valley Mills School where the authors will personally present their books to the second graders and read them aloud to their young audience.

Stahlhut believes in project-based teaching, through which students produce a major piece of work over an extended period of time. The Valley Mills book project, she says, teaches students about the process of writing, oral communication, cooperation, responsibility, meeting deadlines, and the importance of revising, not to mention hard work, self-esteem, and service to others.

Pam Gambill is the other language arts teacher on the team. Twenty-eight years old, she is as at ease with her young students as Stahlhut is.

One of Gambill's strengths, according to Jewel, is that she recognizes that eighth graders are still in many ways children. "She shows us cartoons to sort of bring out the little kid in us again," Jewel told us in her typically perceptive way, "so that we don't feel like we're all grown up. Because, at home, adults seem to think that we can take on everything. Like me. My mom thinks I can take care of myself. Then when I come to school, Ms. Gambill sort of gives me a little leeway to act like a kid again. It makes me feel better. Not so much like I have so much to do and so much to accomplish."

Gambill uses a variety of classroom instruction techniques: she engages students in active discussions, encourages them to express themselves in writing and through art, and uses simulations and role plays to stimulate their thinking. Her quick give-and-take with her students contrasts sharply with Simon's use of vivid description to paint word pictures of major historical events.

Science teacher Leroy Blocher looks like his name; indeed, he played football in college. Now the stocky wrestling coach plays the position of father figure on his team. He is at once soft-spoken yet solid, understated yet strong. One senses that Blocher would run interference for any of his students.

Blocher is a big fan of outcome-based education, or OBE, but he recognizes that it generates considerable controversy among his colleagues. (In recent years, OBE has also come under attack from conservative political and religious groups.) Some swear by it, while others are deeply skeptical. During our visit to Decatur Middle School it seemed to us that there was not any clear consensus among teachers and administrators about what OBE was exactly. Blocher saw it as a way of giving students more chances to demonstrate that they had mastered the material they needed to learn.

Blocher told us that he had attended a national OBE conference in Phoenix during the 1990–91 school year, which led him to realize that he had been doing OBE all along: "I've always given kids second chances on their tests. The only difference now is that I don't take class time to give them the second chance. They have to do that by special arrangement during success period."

"Success period" is a thirty-minute block that begins each day at Decatur Middle School. It is designed to give teachers an opportunity to provide enrichment or remediation to students who need it—to guarantee "success for everyone" (the school's motto). Blocher has posted on the blackboard the names of students who need to make up a test or complete an assignment. During his success period, while most students play cards and socialize, a steady stream approaches him to ask, "Am I okay?" With a paternal smile, Blocher points to the list on the board and says, "If your name's not on the list, you're fine with me."

Blocher acknowledges that many teachers resist OBE because they think it is unrealistic: "They'll say things like, 'Insurance salesmen don't get three chances to make their pitch.' But if we don't get second chances, why did they invent erasers or permit divorces? Eventually, the students will become successful."

The girls on Team 8C all love Jim Crane, the math teacher, and not just because they think he is good-looking. They also appreciate his conviction that every student can succeed in math.

Jewel is in Crane's first-period algebra class. The course is challenging for her, but she gives her teacher high marks. "It's difficult, but he tries to explain it," she said. "He goes slow. He tries to make sure that everybody stays together. That way, nobody is higher than another person. Nobody feels left out or like they're not any good."

Crane's two-year-old son died shortly before our visit, after a long illness. Many of the students on the team mentioned this tragedy and how profoundly it affected them. "Even though he lost his son, he still goes on," Jewel told us with obvious emotion. "His strength gives us the willpower to go on, to finish that algebra class even though it's hard. He's like a model for us. We look up to him a lot because losing a family member is hard. We know that he's having a hard time, but he still comes to school every day. That's the reason that we try to do the best we can for him, and he does the best for us."

What Makes the Team Tick

One of the factors that makes Team 8C work is, not surprisingly, teamwork—spending time together, planning and evaluating shared activities, and regularly talking about individual students' progress. Like other teams at Decatur Middle School, Team 8C meets daily to plan interdisciplinary units, identify and solve problems, and plan special events.

"The primary benefit of teaming," the five teachers asserted in a description of their program, "is the ability to present a core curriculum that interrelates the separate disciplines. We can also be sensitive to the kids through other teachers' eyes." The students we interviewed repeatedly mentioned another element of 8C's success: the teachers on this team take a lot of time to be with their students and help them.

The importance of taking time was evident in a team meeting we observed. The teachers began by going over a list of awards to be given out at the end of the marking period and reviewing a set of upcoming curricular mini-units. Then they turned their attention to a group of students who were acting up in music class. The team decided to do two things. First, they would meet with each of the students involved during their lunch period. Then they would discuss the matter with the music teacher who had reported the problem. In most schools, such problems are handled by administrators, if at all. How many teachers, we wondered, would be willing to use their precious minutes of lunchtime, as these teachers were, to help solve a disciplinary problem in some other teacher's classroom?

Sitting in on these team meetings, we were also struck by the friendly way in which the teachers related to each other and visitors alike, their honesty and self-assurance, and their ability to examine and laugh about past mistakes. Issues were openly discussed, with each teacher getting an equal chance to express his or her point of view. If the group failed to reach consensus on an issue, the majority ruled.

Whether they won or lost the debate, the team members appeared to respect the decision-making process and agreed to abide by the outcome. "We often disagree and argue," one said. "A lot of times, we're outvoted, but we don't pout."

"Yeah," agreed a colleague, "nobody pouts, but one whines." They all laughed.

Getting to Know You

At the start of each school year, the members of Team 8C conduct a three-day orientation for their students before they even hand out textbooks. The teachers use this time to speak individually with every youngster on the team. They tell their students that this is their family, that they are a team, that they need to love and help one another, and that they are all being given a fresh start. Nothing that happened before matters. Now is the time for all of them to succeed.

Always searching for ways to improve, the team decided to enhance its orientation program two years ago by adding a treasure hunt on the school grounds. Teachers divide the students on the team into small groups and send them off in search of various objects hidden around the campus. Teachers and parents are on hand to make sure that the students do not wander too far off, although they are given lots of freedom to pursue their search. According to one team member, "The purpose of this exercise is to teach the incoming students important team values: cooperation, risk taking, and freedom coupled with responsibility."

The team also uses a variety of incentives and rewards. One is the team auction. Each day, the teachers hand out play money with the teachers' pictures on it in return for good behavior or academic performance. Every nine weeks, they use their own real money to buy rewards for the students—candy, puzzles, posters, cakes, and other items. Students get to use their fake money to buy these objects at the auction.

Many educators might frown on this as blatant bribery. (Indeed, extensive research on the use of rewards and incentives shows that they have negative rather than positive effects on students' motivation to learn.) But to Jewel and her classmates these auctions symbolize the teachers' commitment to their students. "They take their own money and buy things like that," Jewel observed, "and the only satisfaction that they get out of it is that we're happy about it."

Every nine-week marking period, the team also takes students to the Pavilion, a nearby recreation center, for a full day of activities. While some students run around the track, lift weights, or play basketball, others talk quietly in small groups. Perhaps most important, teachers and students use this time to make connections. "It's a total fun day," said Jewel. "For some kids it's a chance to let out stress. Just to be able to run."

Interdisciplinary Instruction:
The Pioneer Unit

Over a period of several years, Team 8C has developed a number of interdisciplinary curriculum units that link history, reading, writing, mathematics, and science. Some of these, like the Pioneer Unit, are comprehensive and extend over several weeks. Others are mini-units that typically last for two or three days. Each addresses one or more themes that are both socially significant and relevant to the issues and concerns of young adolescents.

In the Pioneer Unit, students re-create the experience of families who moved west during the American expansion period from 1830 to 1860. While this format is highly engaging, it is not just fun. The Pioneer Unit addresses key curriculum concepts: the hardships experienced by the pioneers, the importance of the westward expansion to the development of the United States, and changes in social roles and responsibilities over time. It also helps students learn the relevance of mathematical and scientific principles in solving real-world problems.

The unit begins with each history class establishing its own wagon train for the simulated journey. Bruce Simon groups the students into families, typically consisting of a husband, wife, and several young children. Husbands are assigned professions of the time: farmer, cattleman, tavern owner, preacher, blacksmith, teacher. Each family has its own wagon and pair of oxen, along with other animals such as horses, cattle, milk cows, and mules.

In each class one boy is elected wagon master by the other boys. The wagon master is responsible for running the wagon train and maintaining harmony among the pioneers. He assigns the other boys in the class to small cooperative groups. Their tasks include establishing a destination (California, Oregon, or Utah); mapping their route from Independence, Missouri, to that destination; drawing a chart depicting the position of every wagon, person, and animal in the wagon train when it is in motion and at rest; and writing out contingency plans in the event of an Indian attack, flood, or drought.

Each girl in the class must list all the items that her family will take on the journey west, taking into account her husband's profession. And she must keep a journal describing the responsibilities and actions of each family member over a twenty-four-hour period. Each task requires careful research and hours of preparation. Boys may choose to help their spouses for extra points.

Some educators might question the team's use of gender-based assignments, but the teachers have deliberately built sex-role differences into the unit to reflect historical facts. Later in the unit, they use these differences as a springboard for discussion about the limited choices that women had in the past and the options available to women today.

While the Pioneer Unit is history centered, it integrates all the other disciplines. In language arts, students read classic American tall tales like "Pecos Bill" and "Paul Bunyan" as well as other fiction such as *Shane* and *The Oklahoma Land Run*. They write their own tall tales, keep daily diaries as they travel west, and compose essays contrasting pioneer times with modern life.

In mathematics, students study volume. Then, using the dimensions of the wagons and the lists of materials generated in history class, they calculate which items can be brought along on the journey. They also calculate how long it will take them to make the trip using a variety of assumptions about distance, rate of speed, and hours per day of travel.

In science, students learn how to preserve food by pickling, make hard candy to be used as throat lozenges, and work in small groups to build aluminum rafts. Students then participate in a "float-off" contest to see which raft can hold the most weight. The unit also integrates the performing arts. For example, the physical education teacher teaches square dancing, while the music teacher introduces Early American music and musical instruments.

Team 8C has refined the Pioneer Unit over the years, and it has been adapted by other eighth-grade teams at Decatur Middle School and beyond. In general, student evaluations have been extremely positive. Students describe it as one of the many ways in which their teachers "make learning fun."

Stories from the Heart: The Dead Poets Society

The students on Team 8C, like young adolescents everywhere, wrestle with a variety of personal, social, and family problems. As they struggle to find their own identity and search for social acceptance, many experience deep feelings of insecurity and depression, while others succumb to pressures from peers to engage in risky behaviors. For some—children of alcoholics, victims of physical or sexual abuse, those living amid urban poverty and violence—the normal developmental challenges of early adolescence can be especially crippling. These groups are at higher risk of suicide.

The teachers on Team 8C believe that these social and emotional issues must be addressed as part of their eighth-grade course of study. They have therefore developed a series of two- and three-day mini-units designed to teach affective skills and help students confront troubling personal problems in a safe and supportive environment.

One of these units, called the Dead Poets Society, is named for the movie of the same name. We have chosen to describe it in detail here to show how some teachers are able to draw on their personal resources to create powerful lessons about life, death, hope, perseverance, and human relationships. While many middle schools set up advisory programs to help teachers establish personal connections with small groups of students, these teachers do it every day in their regular classrooms. For them, issues of adolescent identity, separation, peer pressure, violence, and mental health are part of the core curriculum.

The Dead Poets unit begins with the students watching the film, in which Robin Williams plays Mr. Keating, an iconoclastic teacher in a conservative all-male private school in the late 1950s. Mr. Keating tries to get his students to think for themselves, a radical departure from his school's norms and traditional curriculum. One of his students, Neil, wants desperately to become an actor, but his father insists that Neil must go to Harvard and become a doctor. The conflict eventually results in Neil's suicide, and Mr. Keating, Neil's mentor, is blamed for the tragedy.

After the showing, each teacher conducts follow-up sessions addressing one of five themes: parent-child relations, peer pressure, self-discipline, suicide, and "seize the day" (Mr. Keating's credo). Each session also confronts critical issues facing young adolescents and suggests constructive ways of dealing with them. In order to help students understand that many of their problems are a normal part of growth and development, the teachers talk about their own lives and struggles. These sessions are complemented by informal discussions and opportunities for the students to write about their reactions.

The Dead Poets Society unit is scheduled late in the school year because it requires extraordinary openness and trust between teachers and students. We observed it during a three-day visit to Decatur Middle School in the spring of 1992. The teachers had chosen to show the film on a shortened school day. This way, students could participate in the five follow-up sessions before lunch and go home to think about the experience. This gave the teachers only ten or eleven minutes with each group.

"Seize the Day"

Dee Stahlhut's theme was "seize the day." She began by having her students stand on their desks (an image from the film), looking at poetry and life from a different perspective. Then, with deep emotion, she told the story of her grandmother's death.

"When I think of seizing the day, I think of my grandmother," she said. "She and I were really close, at least as close as my mom and I are now. She and I did a lot together. I did things with her and for her.

"You know, I'm writing my book for my nephew Justin along with you. Justin was my grandmother's first grandchild. And on his first birthday, my husband and I went to her apartment to pick her up to go to his first birthday party."

Stahlhut painfully described the nightmare that followed. When they arrived, her grandmother said she did not feel well and asked them to wait a bit until she felt better. After two hours, Stahlhut knew something was wrong, and she called her parents to come over.

"By that time, her speech was blurred," she continued. "She had had a stroke, but I didn't realize it. She went into the hospital that night, and that was the last time I saw her. I went back the next day to the hospital to see her and she was in a coma. I never talked to her again. I didn't expect her to go like that.

"Everyone in here, we've been close all year. Every day you expect to come here and look around and see each other. You expect to walk in and see the same faces, make the same kinds of jokes, to see me, to see all of us every day. But no one can put a guarantee on life.

"When you're thirteen or fourteen years old, when you're twenty-five years old like I am, even when you're thirty, forty, or fifty—it's hard to think about the fact that you may not be here. And I'm not talking about suicide. I'm talking about an accident or something that comes as a surprise. When I think about seizing the day, I think about not just seizing the day like Charlie [a character in the movie who took reckless chances and got kicked out of school] but living my life so that I get everything I can out of life without hurting anyone else along the way. You must get all you can out of life, knowing that you might not be here and that other people may not be here."

Stahlhut concluded by returning to the movie. She talked about Charlie and the foolish choices that he made. While he thought that he was just being funny, his actions had terrible consequences—he was expelled from school. "Remember," she said, "by seizing the day, Keating didn't mean that they could do anything they wanted and not worry at all. He wanted them to think, too—to think freely and to think clearly."

"You Are Never Alone"

We followed the students to Bruce Simon's class, where most plopped down in a tight circle on the carpeted floor. The lights were off and the room was dark. Simon sat close to his students just outside the circle. A few kids sat at nearby desks, but they were still clearly part of the group.

Simon's theme was suicide, a topic that many educators avoid raising. Indeed, there is mounting concern that, rather than preventing suicide, discussion of the topic may increase the likelihood of suicide ideation and, in the case of extremely troubled youth, action.

Simon talked quietly, and with obvious feeling. The students listened in absolute silence. "I'd like you to sit where you can hear me and see me," he began. "I appreciate your courtesy in watching the show. I understand that it's a powerful show and that sometimes you don't want to watch it. Dead Poets Society has a lot of stuff to offer. Some of it is stuff you don't necessarily want to hear. We look at you kids and we think you're pretty well adjusted, and you think you're doing pretty well yourself. Yet you saw from the film that in spite of appearances, sometimes things aren't real good. Neil's dad did not hate him. Neil's dad was not trying to make his life miserable for him. He was not trying to hurt his son or to ruin his life. He loved the boy. He may not have shown it in a manner that we would appreciate, but he loved his son a lot.

"Some of you have very good home lives; some of you don't. People commit suicide for a variety of reasons. They feel lonely, isolated, or afraid. They feel nobody loves them. They don't have any friends. They're angry. Their heart is broken. Neil had a lot of these feelings, but *Neil had other options*. You each have thousands of options in your life. Choose an option that can help you. Don't choose an option that will end it all.

"One of the things that suicides think is 'I don't have any friends.' Yet when I go to funerals of children who have committed suicide, I can never get up to see the casket because there are so many friends there. Sometimes we don't know what we have. I can't tell you that your lives are going to be wonderful. I can't tell you that everything is going to be all right. I can tell you this: you are absolutely never ever alone. You can come and talk to me today, tomorrow, the year after that, or ten years from now. I will always listen. I may not tell you what you want to hear, but I will listen.

"I understand that you're going through some of the hardest years of your life. The teenage years are very, very, very difficult for you. You argue with your mom and dad all the time, and it frustrates you to death. If you think that your mom and dad hate you because they won't let you do anything, well, let me tell you from a parent's perspective that saying no to your children is the hardest thing you'll ever have to do. You don't say no because you don't love them; you say no because you *do* love them. Discipline is hard.

"Some of you won't open up and share, and I wish you would. I don't care whether you want to cry on my shoulder or slug my shoulder. If you won't talk to me or Ms. Stahlhut, talk to Mr. Crane, talk to Mr. Blocher, or talk to Ms. Gambill. Talk to your mom and dad. Now Neil's dad did not want to hear what he had to say, but Neil needed to talk to him and at least give his dad a chance. You've got to try and talk to your mom and dad, and that may be the hardest thing you've ever had to do.

"We cannot glorify your life or make everything perfect for you at home. We can't make everything perfect for you here. If you mess up here, we may have to chew you out for it, and we will. But that doesn't mean that you are worthless, it doesn't mean you have nothing to offer, and it doesn't mean there is no tomorrow. There is always a tomorrow. I want you to work for it.

"Dead Poets Society is very difficult for us, very personal for us. You go to the funeral of a thirteen-year-old who had everything in the world to live for, and it becomes very personal. We fight very hard. I look around this room, and some of you whom I don't think have any problems have problems. Know that we're here for you tomorrow, forever and a day."

Think for Yourself

In the next classroom, Pam Gambill's topic was peer pressure. In contrast to Simon's impassioned speech, Gambill's session was light and highly interactive. First she invited her students to think about all the different ways in which peer pressure is exerted in the movie. Then she asked them to name various ways in which positive and negative peer pressure is exerted in their own lives. Students called out responses, and the teacher listed them on the blackboard. Jackson's contribution to the list of pressures in the film was "Pressure to think for yourself." Gambill responded, "Jackson, you got the whole idea of the movie."

The class soon created two lists:

Pressure in the Movie

Positive:
to write a poem, be creative
to be in a play
to think for yourself
to call the girlfriend

Negative:
to go to the cave
to drink whiskey
to smoke a pipe
to tell on Mr. Keating
    (to be a narc)

Pressure in Your Life

Positive:
to do your work
to excel both academically
    and behaviorally
to make good grades
to read

Negative:
to smoke
to drink
to do drugs
the "s" word
to steal
to join a gang or a group
to go somewhere you're not
    supposed to go

Gambill seized this opportunity to discuss one of the major challenges of early adolescence: establishing identity.

"Many of you don't want to be yourself right now," she said. "You may dress differently; you may talk differently; you may act differently. You feel silly, because at your age it's extremely important to fit in. But when you get a little older, like in high school or college, you won't feel afraid to be yourself. Your self will just naturally come out. You shouldn't feel afraid to be yourself, even if you don't quite fit in. Because if somebody is your friend, they're going to respect you anyway, whether or not you fit in to what they want you to be.

"I'm an identical twin. It was always very, very hard for me to be myself. When you're raised with someone just like you, it's hard to find yourself. When we got to college, we both started becoming ourselves. She's a lot different than I am. We may look alike and talk alike, but we're each our own person. You can get there if you just try to be yourself and don't be afraid to be different."

Gambill then asked the students to name some ways of dealing with peer pressure. The students called out responses: "Be yourself." "Listen to your parents." "Say no." "Seize the day." "Fit in." Gambill responded: "Fitting in can be either positive or negative, depending on the circumstances. Listening to your parents can also be very hard. A lot of times you don't think your parents know more than you do. At least, I didn't. But it turns out, even though I hate to admit it, that my father was often right. I hated to admit that, and I still won't tell him that. So don't you dare tell him that I said that to you." The students laughed appreciatively.

Tell Dad You Love Him

After Gambill's class, we headed across the hall to Leroy Blocher's room. The bell had rung; we waited impatiently for the previous class to come streaming out. Finally the door opened and students exited somberly in single file. Several boys and girls were wiping their eyes as they passed. What made them cry?

Inside, Blocher told our group that his theme was parent-teen relationships. He reviewed Neil's poor relationship with his father in the film. Then Blocher started to talk about his own family.

"You people have an ideal opportunity to work with your parents, an opportunity I never had," Blocher began. "I was born just prior to Pearl Harbor Day, December 7, 1941, to a lady in Orange County, Illinois. I have no idea who she is, and I never will know who she is. She decided she didn't want me. She was married to a soldier, I guess, and she got pregnant by the soldier. Then that soldier was taken off, and I was left with this lady. She couldn't raise me, so they put me in the Orange County Orphanage, where I lived from 1941 to 1950.

"On Christmas Day, 1950, I was adopted by a couple here in Indianapolis. They came and picked me out of all the kids in the orphanage. They picked me. I had no idea why. I thought I was the luckiest nine-year-old in the world because these two people just came down there and said, 'We'll take that one.'

"My mom and dad who adopted me were fantastic parents—you couldn't ask for any better. They wanted something more for me than what they had. My dad had to drop out of school in the eighth grade to support his two younger sisters while they were in school. When it came time for me to go to school, my dad wanted to make sure I became something."

Blocher told the class, with considerable affection and humor, how his father advised him to become a cobbler or a barber. "If I had followed his advice," he said, "I would have probably been out of work today. But we talked, and we decided that I needed an education. I wanted to go to college, and he thought that was great. But with his income, he couldn't send me to college. So I had to work hard in high school. I got an academic scholarship to Butler University. I played football and ran track, and he encouraged me the whole time. He didn't tell me, like in Neil's case, you have to go to Harvard; you have to be a doctor; you have to make your mom proud.

"We did have problems. My father didn't spend a lot of time talking to me personally. Just four years ago last Friday, on April 17, my dad died." Blocher's voice caught and his eyes filled. There was not a sound in the room. "It's tough for me to talk about this," he continued, "because, after he was dead, my mom and I went through his personal effects. And we found in his effects some pictures of me when I was a baby."

Blocher was crying openly now, and a shock wave went through the room as the kids slowly realized the import of what he was telling them. "He was my real dad. He had come back, nine years later, and picked me out. All along I had thought I was special because this guy had picked me out of the orphanage. But he came back because he was my real father and he felt obligated to come get me. So from 1950 to 1988, thirty-eight years, we lived together. And he didn't think he could tell me, and that hurt. That my dad couldn't sit down and tell me, 'Hey, I'm really your dad, not just your adopted dad.'"

Blocher collected himself a little and went on. "My son and I have a terrific relationship. He teaches here, and he and I coach together. We have a terrific relationship because he and I talk. And that's all I want you guys to do. I want you guys to talk. Don't be afraid to go home tonight, grab Dad, hug him, and tell him you love him. Because I can't do that to my dad now. My son can, and he does—quite a bit."

We filed out of Leroy Blocher's class, wiping our eyes. Looking back over our shoulder, we saw Jewel giving Blocher a hug. When we asked her about it the next day, Jewel said, "He opened up to us and told us things that are hard. Especially that he found out that his adopted dad was really his father after he died. I think he takes that, and, instead of leaning on it and using it as an excuse to be sad and depressed all the time, he uses it as a lesson toward his own son. Now he makes sure that his son knows that he loves him. When he was telling us about this he started crying, and the reaction of all the other kids just showed me that we all do care about each other."

Don't Take the Easy Way Out

Jim Crane's session was last on this first day of the unit. His theme was self-discipline. His session began, like the others, with a reference to the movie.

"Neil was a young man who had everything going for him," said the young math teacher. "Yet he decided that suicide was the only answer. Neil said to his father, 'Okay, I want to tell you how I really feel.' But he couldn't even take another step. Neil couldn't even say another sentence when he was finally ready to tell his father about his passion for acting. Because his father interrupted by saying, 'Now don't start by telling me that you want to be an actor. Don't even start.' And that was the final rejection that Neil could not take any more. But if he hadn't taken the easy way out and lied, things might have ended differently.

"How many of us in our short lives have not had the self-discipline to tell the truth? Have not wanted to face what the real truth was? Ms. Gambill talked to you about drugs. When it comes to drugs, the easy way out is to say, 'Well, everybody else is doing 'em.' Instead of having the self-discipline to say, 'No, I'm not going to do that. I don't care what the consequences of saying no are, I'm not going to do that.'"

Like his colleagues, Crane then told a story about his own life: "There is one other kind of self-discipline I want to talk about. When I was in your shoes, or maybe in ninth grade, I had a guidance counselor who said, 'You know, Jim, we've seen your scores here, and I just don't think that you should try to get a high school diploma that's gonna lead you to college. Because your reading skills are way below everybody else's—two, three, four grades below. And I just don't think that you need to take calculus and college literature and college grammar. You need to go the easy route. Maybe you can go to a trade school. Maybe you can be a plumber or work on a construction site. Your chances of making it in college are one out of a thousand, because you just don't have the reading skills.'

"Well, those two diplomas up there on the wall prove her wrong. It took me five times as long as everybody else to get the work done. It was not easy, and I couldn't have done it if I hadn't had the self-discipline. When everyone else's homework was done and they were having a good time, I was still doing mine.

"This is our third year of doing the Dead Poets Society. We hope that as you graduate from high school and college, you'll say, 'Boy, I remember that day. It made an impression upon me about how hard I had to work to get things done in life.'"

The Day After

Three of the teachers—Dee Stahlhut, Pam Gambill, and Bruce Simon—continued the mini-unit for a second day. They used the opportunity to give students time to talk and write about the film and the themes that were introduced in the follow-up sessions.

Stahlhut began by asking her students to list seven different ways in which people in the movie "seized the day." To kick off what turned out to be a lively discussion, she gave them an example. "Remember Knox giving flowers to his girlfriend in the classroom? That's an example of seizing the day, taking advantage of the moment, daring to be different, daring to strike out and find new ground."

After the kids had talked for a while, Stahlhut gathered her students around her on the floor. "There are times in your life that are really, really difficult to get through, that challenge you to the utmost," she told them. "They make you question sometimes whether you can go on for another day, let alone seize the day and live it to the fullest. I would venture to say that maybe a fourth of you have, at some point in your life, had thoughts of suicide. Not that you would necessarily take it as far as Neil did, but at least you've thought about it.

"If you ever get so down that you even consider suicide, if you ever really start to think about it as an idea or an option, you need to get help. And I don't necessarily mean going to see a counselor or a psychiatrist. You need to tell someone. It's not easy, when life is hard, to do things all alone.

"One way that I get through hard times is to write. Writing is not something you put down so that a teacher can grade it and not something that you need to get every comma, exclamation, and quote right. The importance of writing sometimes is to get out your feelings."

Stahlhut then read an excerpt from her own diary. It begins by describing how upset she gets with her job at times, how emotionally invested she is in her kids, how she was recently moved to tears by reading their autobiographies. "I'm trying to get a grip on blaming myself for everyone else's problems," she read. "A couple of weeks ago, I really got depressed. There are so many people in this world that really need help, and sometimes I feel that I just can't be good enough." She went on to talk about a number of coping strategies that helped her through this difficult period, including reaching out to her family and her colleagues on Team 8C.

Pam Gambill began her second-day session by reading a brief story narrated by a boy who is desperate to be accepted, to have a friend. The friend that he finds, however, leads him into drinking, drugs, and skipping school. The narrator wonders how a friend can make him feel so uncomfortable. What followed was more discussion of peer pressure and techniques for saying no to activities that feel wrong.

In Bruce Simon's class students again had a chance to raise questions about the film and the previous day's sessions. In the discussion, he took every opportunity to draw analogies between what happens in the movie, what happens at school, and what is going on in the students' personal lives. The class talked about the relationship between the father and son in the film, about poetry and romance, about different approaches to teaching, and about the scapegoating of Mr. Keating, the fictional teacher, after his student's death.

Toward the end of class, Simon took a final opportunity to tell the students how much he cared for them and what he expected of them: "We don't ask you to get straight As. We ask you to walk into this class and every class you go into and try. Remember we told you at the beginning of the year that if you would try, we would guarantee you the opportunity to succeed. And I think we've stood by our promise. And I hope that you will remember that when you go to high school, when you go to college, when you get a job, when you get married, when you raise children. We don't expect you to be perfect. We ask you to try, and if you try, and you do the best that you can, then you should be proud of yourself and you should be proud of your accomplishments. If you will do the best that you can, you will never cease to be amazed at the miracles that you will create in your life and those around you."

"We Learn a Lot About Life"

What effect does the Dead Poets Society unit have on the team's students? We talked to several of them afterward. "The most important thing I learned," said Mike, "was that you shouldn't commit suicide because of the people you might hurt around you. Like if you've got a little brother or something and he looks up to you."

"The Dead Poets Society brought up a lot of emotions," said Tammy. "It got us to think about things we don't usually think about. You have a lot of friends, even if you don't know it. We're like a family. If we have a problem, we can go to them. We learn a lot of stuff about life on this team."

To Jewel, the Dead Poets Society unit was one of the highlights of the school year. "We watched the movie, and after the movie our teachers told us things that happened in their own lives," she said. "It was a day to get together and open up our feelings, to take off the mask that everybody shows while they're here at school. Everybody was crying, but some of us were happy. It gave us the chance to let out a lot of stress that we have at home. They give us those opportunities all throughout the year. That's what I think is really special about them. They care. They don't just give us a book and say, 'Read the first twenty pages,' or 'Do the first thirty problems.' They don't like doing it that way because they don't think you're gonna remember anything—and they want you to remember it."

"What 8C Does Should Be Done by Everyone"

Despite the fact that Team 8C accomplished so much with its students, at the time of our visit its approach was neither universally applied nor applauded at Decatur Middle School. We visited two other teams' meetings and found a rather different dynamic from Team 8C's. While the team members seemed comfortable with each other, teachers spent much of their time talking about students who were in academic trouble or, in their words, "messing up." In neither meeting was there much discussion about what the team members could do to help their students succeed.

A respected social studies teacher at Decatur Middle School acknowledged the problem: "My perception is that what 8C does should be done by everyone—equipping children with the tools they need to be successful as students and as members of society. But I don't know if there are that many people in this building, or any building for that matter, that are talented enough, patient enough, or caring enough to do what they do."

The flip side of the teaming story is that, all too often, extraordinarily fine teams—or individual teachers—who serve as pioneers expose the limitations of others. The very fact that they are different and that they begin to attract praise and attention can create envy and resentment among their peers.

We are told that things have gotten better at Decatur Middle School. "What two years ago was a very competitive atmosphere has become one of team building, collaboration, and cooperation," according to Superintendent G. W. Montgomery. "Teams share their strengths; no one team is put up on a pedestal." A member of Team 8C reports that "we are slowly getting past the point where others view us as competitive, unwilling to share, and unwilling to recognize their accomplishments. We do have pride in our team, but that is part of what makes us work hard and get the job done."

John Taylor, who succeeded Wally Bourke as principal in the fall of 1992, attributed much of the competition we observed during our visit to the natural evolution of teaming. "The first stage generally involves widespread resentment of the concept of teaming," he said. "The second stage is competitive, and the final stage is cooperative."

Taylor added that his methods for strengthening teaming at Decatur differed from those of his predecessor. "Wally deliberately praised Team 8C," he said, "and that had both positive and negative effects. While it helped create a vision of what teaming could accomplish, it also fostered jealousy and resentment among other team members."

Taylor said that he and the other school administrators now take great pains to praise all the teams, giving recognition to the teachers and students alike. The principal also schedules grade-level meetings on a regular basis to reduce the insularity of individual teams and encourage schoolwide cooperation. And Taylor has mandated that all teams develop and implement grade-level inter-disciplinary units and otherwise coordinate their activities.

As a result, all the teams in the building have become more active. As each team develops and tests new interdisciplinary units, it shares them freely. Last year, for example, Team 8B implemented an outstanding Career Unit, parts of which Team 8C adopted. And Team 8A has carried out several successful Pioneer Units of its own. In the seventh grade, teams have designed and implemented an engaging Renaissance unit culminating in a Renaissance fair. What Team 8C does is no longer separate and unique at Decatur Middle School.

"We Never Run Out of Love"

What can we learn from Team 8C's experience? One team member summed it up this way: "When we reflected on what makes our team special, we came to the conclusion that it is not the interdisciplinary units, the auctions, Dead Poets, or any single thing we do that makes our team successful. It is primarily the attitude of love and caring we try to provide on a daily basis. Frankly, there are many things about our program we could strengthen; we sometimes run out of time and energy. But we never run out of love."

Team 8C succeeds because the teachers have created a community of shared values: honesty, selflessness, equity, reflectiveness, service to others, and the acknowledgment of each other's pain as well as each other's dignity. Most of all, it has created a community of caring.

This team also provides clear evidence of the transcendent power of stories to convey these values and help young people to find meaning in their own lives. Jackson Fox's story in particular is notable in this era of increasing racial tension in many American schools. The teachers on Team 8C, even though they were all white, acknowledged and respected Jackson's African American heritage. He, in turn, became closely attached to the team and worked hard to live up to its expectations for him.

The stories of Dee Stahlhut, Leroy Blocher, and Bruce Simon also speak to us of the enormous cost of being a truly effective teacher of young adolescents in urban America today. Their strength, ironically, is their vulnerability. Their capacity to touch the hearts of their students depends ultimately on the breakability of their own hearts. Team 8C stands as an example of what teaming can accomplish at the middle school level. It also serves as a reminder—and a warning—of how difficult and fragile such an enterprise can be.

Chapter Five

A Tale of Two Principals

In the preceding chapter, readers met Decatur Middle School's Team 8C. Two principals, Jeff Swensson and Wally Bourke, helped transform Decatur from a relatively unfocused, traditional junior high school into a modern middle school with a clear vision. The story of these two charismatic, thoughtful leaders underscores the importance of careful planning and reflection, using data to drive decision making, and taking risks to bring about change.

The heart of the story, however, is again personalization. Both Swensson and Bourke involved their staff in creating a shared vision, provided formal and informal mechanisms for communication, gave teachers personal support and timely feedback, and helped create a true community of practice. Through their relationships with adults and students alike, they modeled what it means to cherish and respect others, while at the same time setting high standards for performance.

Swensson and Bourke have each gone on to new middle schools and to positions of leadership in the Indiana middle school movement. A new principal, John Taylor, who came to Decatur after our visits to the school in 1992, continues to bring about positive changes. This tale of two, and now apparently three, principals suggests that, given a common vision and faculty support, successful transitions in school leadership are possible.

Jeff Swensson and the Three-Ring Circus

Jeff Swensson became principal of Decatur Middle School in the fall of 1986. He was well versed in the middle school concept, having previously served as assistant principal at a middle school in Cedar Rapids, Iowa. On his arrival at Decatur he immediately initiated sweeping changes.

Social studies teacher Greg Dillon remembers those days fondly. "We had a group of administrators who were energetic and forceful, but not in a mean sense," he said. "Forceful in the sense that they saw their mission and worked very hard at accomplishing it."

Wally Bourke was one of Swensson's two assistant principals. "During those initial stages," Bourke told us, "Dr. Swensson took off running in a hundred different directions—from interdisciplinary teaming, to adviser-advisee, to heterogeneous grouping." Virtually everyone on the staff was involved in the changes.

"I don't know whether he intended to," Bourke added with a smile, "but the end result was that we were coming at teachers with change in so many directions they couldn't unify to resist any of it. They'd gripe about this, that, and the other, but we'd divide and conquer."

There was a method to Swensson's madness. "We were juggling a lot of things—more than three rings of Barnum and Bailey jugglers—but it was all juggling with a genuine purpose and intent," he said. "There were 372 different things that needed to be done, so I just said let's do them."

The frenetic activity provoked criticism and resistance from the faculty. "There was a lot of flack from the teachers," Bourke recalled. "'How can you expect us to do all this?' 'Slow down.' 'Quit pushing us.' 'We're all stressed out.' 'We're going to die.' 'The world's going to end.' We heard that stuff all the time." Some seasoned veterans were so upset by all the changes that they just packed up and left. The majority, however, were energized by this sense of urgency and the impending changes and chose to stay.

Planning Like Crazy

Swensson likens his approach to running a middle school to carrying out qualitative research. "You'd better listen hard and you'd better be real responsive to what's happening immediately, because that has to frame what you do next," he said. "Like researchers," he added, "middle-level administrators must keep their fingers on a lot of pulses, be very well aware of how things are functioning, and then plan like crazy."

At the same time, Swensson recognizes the role that chance plays in the change process. "You have to plan first for stuff that you can plan for and second for stuff that you can't plan for," he told us. "Sometimes incredibly serendipitous things just happen— poof. If they work, that's great. Other things you've really labored and sweated over fall right in the toilet."

Such disappointments, Swensson believes, are not really a problem. Problems come from not experimenting and not working to resolve things when they go awry. "You've got to approach things with the sense of 'We're going to problem-solve the daylights out of this,' and then do it again tomorrow," he said.

One serendipitous thing that happened soon after Swensson arrived was that the Lilly Endowment awarded Decatur Middle School an MGIP planning grant. Immediately the principal set up two different planning groups.

He asked one group to complete the Middle Grades Assessment Program (MGAP), the comprehensive needs assessment process developed by Gayle Dorman at the Center for Early Adolescence. To carry it out, the group interviewed everyone—teachers, parents, and students—about various aspects of the school, including climate, curriculum and instruction, scheduling, and support services. The findings provided the data on which the school based its recommendations for change. The two strongest recommendations were (1) creating interdisciplinary teams and (2) eliminating tracking of students by achievement level.

Swensson described the MGAP process as "the piston on the drive engine that got the whole locomotive running." It engaged the vast majority of the professional staff "in looking at the internal data, to go along with the theory and the research that we'd garnered from external sources," he said. "The MGAP pretty much covered the waterfront. It gave us a common language."

Swensson's real purpose in completing MGAP was teacher "empowerment," a word he believes is overused and often misunderstood. In his view, empowerment involves "thinking about what kids need, what's working, what needs improvement, and what we are about." He knew that he was embarking on an experiment, but he believed that the experiment had to be intentional. "Experiments don't always turn out the way you think," he said. "I mean, outcomes can vary. But I don't believe in turning things upside down without a purpose."

For Swensson that purpose was improving outcomes for children. He believes firmly that those engaged in school reform must be able to answer questions such as these: Are students able to interact with others? How do they think? What do they feel about themselves? Are they capable of solving problems and responding to the world as they find it? Can they serve others? Do they have respect for others?

At the same time that staff members were conducting this formal assessment, Swensson established a six-member school improvement advisory team to help develop the proposal to the endowment. Their assignment was less formal, but equally important: "To fish."

Bourke described their role: "We'd bring people in just to ask them, 'What do you think? Tell us what you want to do. Tell us what you see down the road.' We engaged people in conversations, and we took all kinds of notes." From these informal conversations the advisory team got a feeling for what the staff really wanted to do.

Out of all this research and group activity the seeds of transformation were sown. "Dr. Swensson pulled these two teams together," said Bourke, "and suddenly middle school teaming was popping up all around us. I think it was a deliberate strategy on his part."

Jeff Swensson's Legacy

The resulting changes were quite simply remarkable. "When Jeff first arrived," Bourke recalled, "the teachers in this school had a reputation across the district as rabble-rousers and rowdies. They were the ones who packed meetings when there was some controversy going on. They were the ones who led the teachers' association—and still do. They probably had a great deal to do with the departure of at least two principals."

Bourke believes that Swensson helped change all that. "He did a lot to redirect the teachers' image as rebels into the image of being out front of education," he said. "And I think it was one of the real keys to this group as a whole. Suddenly, we were no longer being the rowdies; we were the people doing the right stuff, despite what the system told us was right. We were throwing off the shackles of the system and pursuing improvement on our own."

"It was a school filled with exceptionally good people," said Swensson. "That's where you've got to begin no matter what. I think it was also a school that was kind of demoralized. There really had not been much focus on students prior to my arrival—as a building issue, that is. And I think that people were very much ready for change and, in some cases, very knowledgeable about it. I certainly didn't bring this tremendous gift. I wouldn't ever say, 'I saved you all.' That was not the case. But there wasn't energy that was coordinated, focused, and attuned to the application of good ideas about middle-level education."

After three years of creating a shared vision and initiating change, Swensson announced to a dismayed faculty and student body that he was leaving. He moved to Stony Brook Middle School in Warren Township, where, as principal, he continued to exercise his considerable leadership skills. (He has since moved to Raymond Park Middle School, also in Warren Township.) He also was elected president of the Indiana Middle Education Association and remains a strong force for middle-grades reform across the state.

We asked Swensson why he left Decatur Township. He replied that he had a disagreement with the superintendent and would not elaborate. But he clearly felt that the disagreement was serious enough to warrant his resignation: "As a subordinate and member of the team, I felt it was unethical for me to remain in my position if I could not support the direction, decisions, or style of my immediate superiors."

Swensson left behind a considerable legacy. "Jeff motivated people," a member of Decatur's Team 8C told us. "He was all over the building. He didn't issue directives or conduct formal evaluations. He was here, there, and everywhere. He knew as much about the building as anyone. He was a great grant writer. He didn't mess around. He knew what he wanted and worked hard to get it. He pushed and motivated teachers."

He also knew how to mentor and support his assistant principals, grooming them to take on leadership positions. "All of us worked together closely," Swensson said. "My premise is that every assistant principal will be a principal some day. Maybe not in this building—leaders often go on to other responsibilities. So we need to share leadership.

"It's not a book that you pass along. It takes time to develop leadership. I do remember two things that we did intentionally. First, every Friday afternoon I would sit down with the two assistant principals over a Pepsi. It might take twenty minutes or two hours, depending on the week. We'd use that time to discuss what we'd accomplished and where we were heading. This was in addition to all our other formal meetings.

"Second, in the summer, when the building was empty, we spent a lot of time together. We used that time to set goals and to figure out who would take responsibility for what. We'd ask ourselves, 'What is middle-level education? What's best for our students? How can we support both students and colleagues? How do we carry forward our vision of achievement and excellence?'"

Bourke put it this way: "It didn't take me long to fall under the charm of Jeff Swensson. A lot of it stems from the fact that he's such a dynamic person. It's difficult to work with him and not learn something from him. Not wanting to be left behind, I had to pick things up quickly. So I started searching out school literature, everything I could get my hands on. I felt I had to stay one step ahead of all the groups we had put in place."

Bourke succeeded Swensson as principal of Decatur Middle School. His fellow assistant principal, Jim Rubush, went on to become the highly respected principal of Kesling Middle School in LaPorte, Indiana.

Wally Bourke: Working Through Relationships

More than six feet tall, dark-haired, of medium build, Wally Bourke resembles John Wayne in his younger days. He is outgoing, charming, and witty. After Swensson left for Stony Brook, Bourke managed to implement many of the changes his predecessor had set in motion during his short tenure. At the same time, Bourke established his own style and carved his own record of accomplishment at Decatur. Like his mentor, Bourke became a leader in the Middle Grades Improvement Program Network and the Indiana Middle Level Education Association.

When we asked Bourke to describe his leadership philosophy, he replied, "Working through relationships with people—knowing who those people are, what they want, and what they need. I think you build structures around those things. Then you get people to be a part of those structures because of the relationship you have with them."

Bourke builds relationships with staff and students alike. Walking down the hallway with him, we were struck by the way students teased this principal who towered over them. Their familiarity almost bordered on disrespect. Some poked him playfully and said, "Hi, Wally!"

Later, when we mentioned these observations to Bourke, he said, "That's something that grows out of teaming. A lot of the reason they poke at me is because I poke at them. To be truthful, I enjoy it tremendously. I don't think it borders on disrespect. The 'Wally' bit kind of gets to me, but I don't see that as threatening, although I don't want them to make a habit of it.

"When I walk through the halls, I make a point to see how many kids I can touch—a pat on the back, or any way to make contact with them. And they feel free to do the same to me. I think it gives me a certain rapport with those kids. Then, when they're in need, they feel free to come see me. And when they're in difficult situations and they want to stomp and kick, I know it's not directed at me."

Creating a Shared Vision

Bourke is not afraid of articulating a vision and then working to see that others share that vision. Dee Stahlhut, one of the language arts teachers on Team 8C, caught us one day as we walked past her classroom. She wanted to make sure that we understood the importance of Bourke's progressive philosophy to her as a young teacher.

When she was a student teacher in another community, she told us, she frequently heard comments like "Don't smile until November." Her colleagues feared that, being young and inexperienced, she would lose control of her classroom if she tried to befriend students. During her initial interview with Bourke, she quickly learned that his philosophy was exactly the opposite—and much like her own. He told her that good student behavior is the product not of impersonal relationships but of mutual respect, trust, and bonding. "So," said Stahlhut, "it was a good feeling coming on board."

Marilyn Bunner, chair of the social studies department and a member of Decatur's School Improvement Council, also talked about Bourke's vision. "Wally truly wants what is best for this school," she said. "He wants this to be a place where children can learn, where children can enjoy what they're doing, where they can be encouraged to be the absolute best that their God-given talents can make them be. He wants a faculty that is happy, motivated, and has the latitude to grow."

"Frequently we know where we want people to go," Bourke told us. "The key is to create the perception that they're making their own decisions about how to get there." Though he laughed when he said this, it is a serious statement. When he says it to other principals, they sometimes accuse him of being manipulative. But it is hard to believe that Decatur's seasoned and independent-minded staff could be manipulated by Bourke or anyone else. In truth, under Bourke's leadership they had a great deal of power and shared much of the responsibility for decision making.

Sixth-grade teacher Jan Knight recalled one of several incidents where Bourke went to extraordinary lengths to involve his staff in critical decisions. She and the other sixth-grade teachers were reintegrated into the middle school in the fall of 1991. Knowing how important the composition of interdisciplinary teams can be, Bourke actively sought their advice in making his assignments. Before school started, he assembled all the new staff members and asked them to write down the names of people they preferred as team members, as well as anyone with whom they really did not want to be teamed. Once he had assembled the information, he sent out a skeleton plan to each team member requesting feedback. According to Knight, several people took advantage of this opportunity to suggest changes. While he could not honor all their requests, he made every effort to take teachers' preferences into account.

Providing Instructional Leadership

Bourke is not just charismatic and personable; his knowledge of teaching and learning is considerable. During our conversations he spoke with great insight about the connections between teaming, changes in scheduling, and innovative approaches to curriculum and instruction.

Bourke noted that teaming encourages teachers to look at their practice in new ways; it also helps to reduce isolation. The team schedule provides members with time to meet as a group, visit each others' classrooms, and develop and implement interdisciplinary projects. The more flexible schedule also provides greater opportunities for teachers to attend professional development activities. At Decatur Middle School, teachers have taken advantage of such opportunities to learn about time on task, cooperative learning, and teaching for diverse learning styles. Bourke spoke with pride of the changes that had occurred in curriculum and instruction under his and Swensson's tenure. At the same time, he was quick to point out specific areas in which additional staff development was needed.

"Almost all of our teachers have some focusing activity ready for our kids as soon as they walk in the door," he said. "Their objectives, if they're not written on the board, at some point have been clearly stated so that kids know what their intended actions are, what they're going to learn, and how they're going to demonstrate those learning functions.

"It's not unusual to see very well run cooperative learning activities. It's not unusual to see very poorly run cooperative learning activities, either. We have some teachers who still think group work is cooperative learning.

"We have trained all of our teachers in learning styles, and it's not atypical to see them reaching for different learning styles, which is probably the easiest thing to incorporate. Many of them really vary the activities in their classrooms. We push proximity to kids and moving about classrooms to the hilt. With the exception of some of our older teachers, whose legs are literally giving out, you very seldom see them behind a desk or behind a podium. They are out in the middle of the classroom."

Our classroom observations tended to support Bourke's perceptions, although we also found considerable variability. Some teachers used a variety of innovative teaching methods: cooperative learning groups, hands-on activities, interdisciplinary units, multimedia, and the like. Others relied heavily on textbooks and lectures.

Many of the curricular changes at Decatur Middle School came about as the result of Superintendent G. W. Montgomery's emphasis on outcome-based education, or OBE. "OBE fits in beautifully with the middle school philosophy," Montgomery told us. "It complements structural changes such as teaming and scheduling, because it emphasizes individual students and their success.

"The primary thing that OBE does is help teachers look at kids in different ways. It sets high expectations for students. It says to them, you will learn and we will do whatever it takes to help you get there—no matter how long it takes. It produces a more cooperative environment. It also encourages kids to take more responsibility for their own learning."

Not everyone at Decatur Middle School agreed with the superintendent's views. Many felt that, unless implemented properly, OBE can be relatively mechanistic and counterproductive. Teachers can wind up spending a great deal of time ensuring that students achieve 80 percent mastery on essentially trivial facts and rote skills.

Yet Decatur Middle School did introduce a number of classroom practices designed to meet the overarching goal of OBE: linking instruction to carefully specified outcomes. One of these was Madeline Hunter's approach to teaching and learning. Bourke commented, "This is, in essence, 'best shot' instruction." Teachers use a variety of methods to give students every chance to succeed: experiential activities, formative tests, practice, enrichment, and expanded opportunities for learning outside the classroom.

Another practice that grew out of the superintendent's emphasis on OBE was the thirty-minute success period that began each school day. Bourke described success period as "a time for kids to go back to teachers to get help, or to meet with teachers where they may need to take a test, do correctives, or follow-up on enrichment. It's also supposed to be a time for the implementation of the adviser-advisee program, which we still do very poorly."

At the time of our visit, there was general consensus that the adviser-advisee program needed improvement. As social studies teacher Greg Dillon commented, "We have a program, we have a handbook, we have activities—but these are all fun and games. The program includes too many inconsequential activities that really don't speak to our students' needs."

Decatur Middle School was not unique in this regard. Many middle schools have had trouble implementing student advisory programs, largely because most middle school teachers are uncomfortable outside their traditional role as instructors. At the end of the 1992 school year, the Decatur School Improvement Council created a task force to examine the adviser-advisee program and suggest ways to strengthen it.

Shared Decision Making

Like Jeff Swensson, Bourke believes strongly in shared leadership. During his tenure at Decatur Middle School, he established two standing committees that aided him in managing and setting direction for the school.

The school management team consisted of a broad-based group including the principal, the media specialist, all the department chairs, and a representative from every team that did not have a department chair on it. At monthly meetings this team helped Bourke address basic administrative issues: Are we going to change the bells? Where are we going to spend our money? Who is developing the budget? Marilyn Bunner, a member of the management team, described its operation this way: "We discuss all sorts of things. Anything that comes to mind that would enable us to run an effective building and, more important, assist the kids to be successful."

Bourke also set up a School Improvement Council composed of the management team plus some parent representatives that also met monthly. He described its purpose as "seeking out new adventures in school improvement." Members were responsible for answering the following questions: Are we really doing what we have been saying we are doing? What do we do to get better? What direction are we going to go?

Council members also oversaw the expenditure of MGIP funds, supervised the collection and analysis of MGAP data, and monitored the MGIP grant. In addition, Bourke asked the council to identify staff development needs and recommend programs for the four staff development days set aside by the district each year.

As specific issues arose, Bourke created ad hoc committees to assess the problem and propose solutions. One such committee was asked to examine the adviser-advisee program, as noted earlier. Another such committee, the discipline task force, was established to examine high rates of suspensions and expulsions at Decatur and to recommend ways of reducing them.

"Talk-About" Sessions and "Listening Posts"

Bourke used a variety of informal communication mechanisms to gather and impart information, test ideas, and learn what was on teachers' minds. He believed in the importance, he said, of "pressing flesh with teachers, being in team meetings, and building the relationships that really make a school go."

One strategy Bourke favored was holding "talk-about" sessions for anybody who wanted to talk. He would also schedule a "listening post" either after school or during the day. During these times he would sit in an accessible spot—the conference room or media center—and listen to whoever came by with something to say.

"The conversations varied from griping about school procedures, like how grades are completed, to suggestions for curriculum revisions," said Bourke. "Many teachers have great ideas or substantive complaints that they are reluctant to share. Listening post provided a good motivation for them to share things they might not otherwise."

Bourke and his fellow administrators were very visible, acknowledged sixth grade teacher Jan Knight. "He comes over here and walks the hall," she said. "I've been in buildings before where the administrators came in and closed their doors. You were lucky if you could catch them for a meeting of any kind during the day. Here, nine times out of ten, if you go into the office, although some doors may be closed because administrators are working with students, there is always some door open. There's good communication."

When he wanted his faculty to move in a certain direction, Bourke was also willing to use his office as a kind of bully pulpit. He would stuff teachers' mailboxes with articles and preach to team at faculty meetings. Most teachers admired his zeal and commitment, although a few complained that he sometimes pushed too hard.

Using Data for Decision Making

Like Jeff Swensson, Bourke is an advocate of using data to inform decision making. More than three years into the change process, he asked the School Improvement Council to repeat the MGAP assessment in preparation for the school's second MGIP grant proposal. Greg Dillon worked with about a dozen other teachers, a PTA person, and a consultant from Indiana State University to carry out the second assessment. The committee interviewed every adult in the building, as well as twenty-five students and fifty parents. "One of the reasons we chose MGAP," said Dillon, "was that we felt that the staff would take ownership, and for the most part that's been true."

After the interviews had been completed, the committee brainstormed strengths and weaknesses and came up with recommendations. "We were pretty critical of ourselves," Dillon said. Based on the results, the committee made the following recommendations: improve the school's relationship with the community, increase parental involvement, re-examine the "flex period" (the precursor to success period), set limits, and work harder to promote students' confidence and academic achievement.

Bourke also used formal teacher evaluations as an opportunity to reinforce effective teacher behavior and stimulate change. By visiting teachers' classrooms, attending team meetings, and generally taking the pulse of the school, he was able to identify both staff strengths and needs. "Wally was outstanding in my first year with his encouragement and his evaluations of me," Dee Stahlhut told us. "That helped me more as a teacher than anything else because of my positive start and the confidence that he instilled in me."

Giving Credit to Others and Acknowledging Limitations

Another leadership strategy that Bourke uses is giving others ample credit. He was quick to praise his predecessor, whom he referred to affectionately as "the venerable Dr. Swensson." Bourke also spoke highly of the Decatur faculty. When we praised Cathy King, an exemplary seventh-grade language arts teacher, he commented, "She can do anything. I thought I was a great teacher until I got to observe some of the classrooms in this building."

Bourke also expressed humility about Decatur Middle School and its accomplishments to date. After we told him how highly the school was regarded among the members of the MGIP Network, he quickly pointed out that the school still had serious problems.

"I hear this stuff periodically," he said. "'Gee, aren't we great?' and 'Is that where you work?' Let me give you the negative view of our school, because we do have faults. We've got major things we really need to work on. Yes, we've made great headway in terms of scheduling, and in terms of the way we deal with kids in an affective manner, and communication with parents and a lot of other things.

"But there are two key things that we have not done. We have not changed the quality of the interaction between our adults and kids—not to the level that I expect, anyway. We still have too many teachers who have an us-versus-them mentality, and we're not willing to go out and do what it takes to be the nurturing adults that adolescents really need. Second, we're still throwing kids out of here too fast. Our suspension and expulsion rate is higher than I would like for it to be."

Circumventing the System

Bourke did not always walk a straight line in getting from here to there. When he could not change district or school policy directly, he attacked it from another direction—by changing practice. For example, according to state law and local district policy, corporal punishment is still permitted in Decatur Township. But during his last years as principal, the practice was virtually eliminated at Decatur Middle School.

When asked whether youngsters were ever paddled at his school, Bourke explained, "It still exists as a policy; we just don't do it. I think that, three or four years ago, we swatted ten or fifteen kids. I think we paddled one kid last year. We suspended him a few times, and he was having all kinds of problems, and Mom and Dad were up in arms that we never paddled him. We gave him a swat. It did him no good, and it was my last swatting.

"It's sneaky," Bourke continued, "but it's the way we've changed a great deal of things. We change them, and then we change the policy later. Basic classes are still a part of our curriculum. We've got 'em, but there are just no kids in them. We just don't schedule any-one into them. We did the same thing with corporal punishment."

In one sense, this approach was highly effective. During Bourke's tenure as principal, he managed to introduce radical changes at Decatur Middle School without having to take on either the school board, the central office, or the teachers' union directly. But it also created problems.

When we asked Pat Rumble, the school's at-risk counselor, what she would do to address the social problems at the school, she said, "I would like to eliminate corporal punishment." When we told her that we thought corporal punishment had already been eliminated at Decatur, she was taken aback. "I wasn't aware of that," she said. "The kids still think they can be paddled."

By not addressing the policy issue directly, Bourke created confusion among his faculty and left students feeling anxious. He also left open the possibility that other administrators, with a different perspective, could take matters into their own hands. Indeed, we found some evidence that students were being paddled at school without Bourke's knowledge. Finally, his tactics created the potential for conflict with his superiors in the school system.

A Difficult Decision

When we visited Decatur Middle School in the spring of 1992, Bourke was looking for another job. After four years at the helm, he was ready for another challenge. He also felt that he did not have the full support of the central office, and he was in serious conflict with one assistant superintendent about staffing and other issues. He admitted that it was one of the hardest decisions he has ever made.

Many of the staff members we interviewed during our visit reported that things were adrift and that communication had broken down at the school, yet few knew the reason why. "I think the atmosphere has changed," said Stahlhut. "I'm guessing that Wally, like the rest of us, is feeling swamped right now. I look forward to next year. I think communication's the key. That's where we're lacking right now."

Looking back, Bourke admitted that things were at a turning point during our visit. Having spent the first part of the year dealing with the new building and integrating the new sixth-grade staff, his management systems were a bit frayed at the edges. Knowing that he was about to leave, Bourke had also let several of his informal communication mechanisms lapse. He had not had a listening post or talk-about session in a long time, had not attended many team meetings, and had kept to his office more than in prior years. Even his formal meetings were irregular during this period, which added to the feeling of isolation in the building. "I didn't spend enough time with my staff," he said. "I didn't spend enough time pressing the flesh with these people. Had I stayed on, the thing that would have been highest on my priority list would have been the people in the building."

At the end of the school year, Bourke announced his resignation to a tearful faculty. With his departure, the school lost its second outstanding leader in six years. Bourke became principal of Fall Creek Valley Middle School, a brand-new (some might say palatial) school in Lawrence Township just north of Indianapolis.

The Role of MGIP

We asked both Bourke and Swensson how the Middle Grades Improvement Program affected Decatur Middle School. Bourke replied, "I think the real key to change in schools is discretionary money. So when a teacher walks in the door and says, 'I've got to go to this workshop. This is the guru I have loved all my life. He can teach me things that I can come back and share with other people'—I can send him. The guy across the street can't."

In addition to sending staff to conferences, Bourke used the funds to purchase many things that were essential to bringing about change: equipment, planning time, release time, books, and materials. Despite their critical importance, Bourke admitted that these things "are simply too doggone tough to get through a regular school budget." He continued, "I think eventually we would have gotten there, but it would have taken a lot longer and it would have been a lot tougher.

"We had one teacher in particular who hated this 'open' stuff. I told this guy that I was going to send him to some conference—I don't remember what it was—and that I wanted him to be the expert when he came back. He went away to this conference, and he hasn't been the same guy since he came back. It was just as if someone had flipped the switch. If I hadn't had the money to send him there, it would have never happened. We've done that a number of times."

Asked how this teacher had changed, Bourke replied, "This teacher was more influenced by the fact that he was being asked to be a leader than by the content of the in-service training he received. It was his empowerment and feeling of authority and respect that made the difference for him. He felt valued and began to contribute and behave accordingly."

Over time, teachers had less need for this kind of staff development, as they became more reflective practitioners. During our visit, we met many teachers who were actively engaged in self-renewal. For example, seventh-grade language arts teacher Cathy King and four other teachers had just returned from a workshop on portfolio assessment and writing workshop techniques. They could hardly wait to share what they had learned with their peers at their regularly scheduled department meeting. With King and her colleagues serving as facilitators, the teachers discussed the limitations of traditional paper-and-pencil tests, the need for more "authentic" assessment practices, and the advantages of introducing projects at the middle school level. At the end of the meeting, many of those present agreed to try the new methods in their classrooms and report back at the next meeting.

Swensson described MGIP as the major catalyst for middle school reform throughout the state. "I truly believe that good work is legion in a lot of places," he said. "But we needed, certainly in poor old Indiana, a coalescing, a sort of call to arms. And I believe that call was issued, and continues to be issued, in the form of the support from the endowment and the important ripple effects that has generated. Witness the MGIP Network and the Indiana Middle Level Education Association.

"There's just a lot of things that have developed. Some were intentional, and others just managed to spring up. And that's neat. That's very much part of what happens in the middle-level school—again, the intentional school. This is a controlled effort to realize a profound and vital goal."

Postscript

Decatur Middle School had come a long way during the six years that Swensson and Bourke, with the support of MGIP, served as principals. Yet when he departed at the end of the 1991–92 school year, Bourke left behind some daunting challenges for his successor.

As the preceding chapter showed, not all the teams in the school had coalesced as had Team 8C, and jealousy among the teams had arisen. Although corporal punishment had apparently been greatly reduced, suspension and expulsion figures remained extremely high, especially for minority students. Indeed, because of the seriousness of this problem, Bourke had set up a disciplinary task force to look into the problem and recommend solutions. And, as in many other middle schools across the country, the quality of curriculum and instruction demanded more attention.

The district found a capable successor in John Taylor, who had been assistant principal at Decatur Central High School. Taylor has built on and strengthened the work of those who went before. "Because schools are dynamic places," said Superintendent Montgomery, "it should come as no surprise to know that the climate of the building has changed dramatically since the departure of Wally Bourke and Jeff Swensson—for the better, I might add."

A member of Team 8C agrees: "John Taylor continues the flow of good principals at Decatur Middle School. He is well versed in the middle school philosophy, and he has worked hard to improve the work of the teams in the building and the cohesiveness of the staff in general. He has changed the outlook of the sixth-grade teachers, creating an environment where they feel much more part of the middle school. Like Wally, John allows us to be risk takers and is a risk taker himself. It didn't take him long to earn our team's respect."

Barbara Jackson, director of the MGIP Network, feels that John Taylor may have been just what Decatur Middle School needed after Bourke left. "Jeff set the vision and got people to buy in," she said. "Wally is an implementer. He is very forceful; he calls the shots.

John is an unexpected pearl. His quiet leadership has led to teacher empowerment. His style is laid-back, but he is quite accessible."

Taylor himself said, "My strength is in fine-tuning." This modest answer epitomizes his behind-the-scenes but highly effective leadership style. He has, in fact, achieved three major accomplishments since taking over as principal of Decatur Middle School.

First, he has worked hard to create one school out of nine teams, three grade levels, and the two wings of the building. As noted in the preceding chapter, he took several steps to reduce competition and promote collaboration among all the schools' interdisciplinary teams. In addition, he significantly modified the sixth-grade schedule so that the teams had more planning time. In this way, he "created equity in the two ends of the building."

Second, he has taken steps to become fully "inclusive"—that is, to provide appropriate teaching and learning experiences for students with disabilities in regular classrooms. As of this writing, Taylor had fully integrated students with learning disabilities; he was still working on integrating the emotionally disabled and the mildly mentally disabled.

Third, he has worked closely with his faculty to improve the advisory program. "Basically, we sat down one summer and developed a schoolwide program," he reports. "We identified themes for each six-week grading period and at least one schoolwide activity for that same period. We also developed a resource guide that contained a number of additional activities that teachers could choose at their own discretion."

The themes and schoolwide activities helped set direction and provided a structure for the adviser-advisee program. But Taylor recognized that the materials alone would not be sufficient to change teacher practice. So he also uses faculty meetings to provide training for teachers. During these sessions, which last only fifteen or twenty minutes, teachers who served on the development team discuss the theme for the coming grading period, model the schoolwide activity, and suggest additional implementation ideas.

While Taylor acknowledged that the training is not very intensive, he feels "it has made teachers feel more comfortable with the adviser-advisee program, which is working much better now."

Decatur's story illustrates once again that change is never-ending. Even schools that are pioneers of change need constant attention and continual renewal. Decatur is also an example of the role played by transformational leaders in bringing about and maintaining school improvement. It suggests that strong leaders can successfully pass the baton to others and that different leadership styles may be equally effective. Still, the high turnover of principals at Decatur Middle School tells a cautionary tale for district administrators about the need to give such leaders their full support.

Chapter Six

Moving the System

The sixth-grade language arts class at Portage Middle School on the west side of Fort Wayne seemed remarkably relaxed and informal. (Admittedly, this was during the schoolwide "enrichment and review" period, the last block at the end of the day, which is designed to allow kids to let off some steam.) But the people in this school looked happy. The moment we walked in we were greeted by the kids: "Hi! Who are you? What are you doing?" When we said we were visiting from out of town to observe some classes, they instantly volunteered their opinion: "This is a good school."

The class was full of movement and activity, but not at all chaotic. Kids were talking and working together in small groups. They were playing a spelling game, with the class divided into two teams. Debbie Hudson, the teacher, was warmly supportive of every child, full of encouragement and energy. She clearly loved what she was doing.

Later we sat in, unannounced, on a joint math-science curriculum planning session of the sixth- and eighth-grade teams. (Like Sarah Scott Middle School in Terre Haute, Portage Middle School had just one team per grade level because of its relatively small size—524 students at the time of our visits.) Again, what was immediately striking about the scene was that the people in the room were obviously having fun. Nine teachers were brainstorming ideas for interdisciplinary units and they were acting a lot like middle school students on a break—making jokes and wisecracks, kidding each other, arguing. But they were also getting the work done.

One teacher was running the meeting, writing the group's ideas on the board and keeping it on track. They had come up with a bunch of catchy names for their math-science units—"Where in the World?" "Gee, I'm a Tree" (a play on *geometry*), "Water Water Everywhere," "Shake Rattle and Roll" (a unit on earthquakes and volcanoes)—but they also talked about whether there was real substance behind the fun titles and about the logical connections and continuity among the units. Part of the discussion was about connecting the units to community service projects, such as having the earthquake-volcano unit involve getting the students to participate in disaster planning in the community.

Arleen Zumbrun, a Fort Wayne Community Schools central office administrator whose area includes Portage, accurately summed up our own impressions of this school when she told us, "It's a happy place. Kids are busy."

A Rapid Transition

Eleven middle schools are located in the Fort Wayne district. We could have chosen any number of these schools to highlight because the story of middle school change in Fort Wayne was unique among the communities we studied. Here, the central administration played an essential supporting role, providing both leadership and the financial resources needed to help all schools over time. It also introduced teaming and other key features of the middle school model.

What is most remarkable about the high level of positive energy we found among both teachers and students at Portage is the fact that, at the time of our visits in the spring of 1992, the school was in its very first year of interdisciplinary teaming and in the midst of a second major organizational change: a shift to a schoolwide curricular focus on math and science, as part of a citywide school choice program. Moreover, because of a teachers' contract dispute, the Portage staff had never carried out the Middle

Grades Assessment Program that was so valuable in setting goals and changing teachers' attitudes at other MGIP schools like Sarah Scott and Decatur.

Yet, in spite of circumstances that would have certainly hindered the process of change at many other middle schools, the Portage staff was moving ahead full steam, eager to collaborate and to learn. Interdisciplinary teaming had become an integral part of the school program in just one year. Virtually everyone with whom we spoke—counselors, teachers, parents, and students—praised the effects of this change. Teaming was credited with producing a significant reduction in disciplinary problems and referrals to the central office.

The elements of this successful and rapid transition to school-wide interdisciplinary teaming were, first of all, a young, energetic, child-oriented faculty predisposed to experimentation; an articulate veteran principal, Chuck Hoffman, who came to Portage in 1990 with valuable experience as a leader in the middle-grades reform movement in Indiana and with a clear vision of what needed to happen at the school; the coherent and well-designed blueprint for change in the central office of the Fort Wayne Community Schools; and, finally, the technical and financial resources made available through the Lilly Endowment's Middle Grades Improvement Program.

An unusual and noteworthy element of the team design at Portage is its "related arts" team, made up of the teachers of home economics, industrial arts, physical education, music, fine arts, and a special "adolescent skills" course. Together, they form a fourth interdisciplinary team to complement the sixth-, seventh-, and eighth-grade teams. At other schools we visited, the teachers of these subjects often felt marginalized—shut out of the larger teaming effort. At Portage, they are among the most vocal supporters of team teaching.

Another strength of Portage's program is its emphasis on preventive guidance. Counselor Betsy Gemmer works with students and teachers to prevent various high-risk behaviors involving guns and violence, teen pregnancy, and suicide. In addition, well-conceived curricular units on sexual and other forms of physical abuse are integrated into Patricia McKinney's adolescent skills program.

Community service projects are an important component of the program. Seventh-graders have worked as peer tutors with students in the sixth grade at Portage as well as with younger children at the Lindley Elementary School. Other students have built benches for use by the elderly in two nearby city parks, cleaned up the park grounds, and painted playground equipment. Other service projects have included collecting canned food for a local food bank and toiletry items for clients of the Mental Health Association's outreach program.

Finally, the parents we spoke to were uniformly supportive of the school and its recent changes. They appreciated the school's new homework hotline, a telephone message system that gives them access both to their children's homework assignments for that night and to general school information. And we were impressed by the huge turnout at a Mother/Grandmother Breakfast held in the school cafeteria one morning—one of several efforts to build connections with Portage students' families.

Fort Wayne: Decline and Turnaround

Portage's students, taken together, are not quite as mired in poverty and isolation as those at Harshman or Sarah Scott, and the school does not draw a sizable group of students from an inner-city neighborhood of concentrated poverty as Decatur Middle School does. But Portage is unquestionably an urban school, typical of thousands of other middle schools in financially strapped communities across America. At the time of our visits, 18 percent of its students were minorities; 44 percent were eligible for free or reduced-priced meals. And its staff was painfully aware of widespread alcoholism, violence, abuse, and family breakdown in the homes of the children.

"When I came to Fort Wayne," Principal Hoffman told us, "we had 48,000 students and the number was rising. Now we're down to probably 32,000. We've had to close buildings, we've had to tear down buildings, and we've had to lay off a lot of teachers. When you lay off teachers, you know, and then you have an opening in a middle school, you end up having to hire surplus high school teachers who are not trained in middle school education. And it takes a long time to retrain them. If they even want to be retrained.

"We've had an awful lot of setbacks in Fort Wayne," Hoffman added. "I think the major one was the declining enrollment. And then when International Harvester moved out of here, boy, that devastated us. We lost six thousand families overnight. And all of them had school-age kids. We went through some frightful times."

Hoffman thought that things were starting to look up in Fort Wayne at the time of our visits in 1992. He noted that a lot of parents had pulled their children out of the public schools and put them in private ones during the worst times but said "we're getting some of them back now." He had high hopes for William Coats, the new superintendent. "He's very, very dynamic," said Hoffman, crediting Coats with generating a new spirit of enthusiasm among educators in Fort Wayne. "We were just stagnating there for a while," he said. "I hope he sticks around."

A Model of Inclusion

One of Portage Middle School's most significant successes has been its progress in eliminating tracking and in including students with a variety of disabilities in regular classrooms. Eight percent of its students had individual educational plans (IEPs) designed to address various disabilities in the 1991–92 school year, and almost all these children were being taught for at least part of the day in regular classrooms.

Portage is one of three Fort Wayne schools with a special program for emotionally disabled students. A special program is available for hearing-impaired students that includes signing. We observed some of these students in classes; they were not just accepted by the other children but enjoyed considerable communication and interaction with them. In one industrial arts class, a hearing-impaired student had his own sign-language interpreter translating the teacher's instructions for him. We saw, during the individual work period, other students who were obviously not hearing impaired having conversations with this student in sign language.

Tim, a Portage sixth grader, was classified as both learning and emotionally disabled. Around third grade he was diagnosed as dyslexic. "He started to have numerous problems in school," said Amy Daniel, his special education teacher at Portage, "not finishing his work, becoming frustrated easily with the work—and then the frustration led to some classroom outbursts, lots of crying in class. He couldn't control his emotions. He would get into arguments with teachers and other students. So they placed him in an emotionally handicapped class." At Portage, Tim was mainstreamed in untracked social studies, science, and reading classes, and his teachers reported that he was performing well in them. In math, language arts, and spelling he worked with Daniel.

Like other Portage students, Tim introduced himself to us one day. It was during Kathy Amborn's social studies class. The students were giving oral reports on Latin American culture, and we had asked Steven, a student who gave a report on Mexico, where he had gotten his information.

"From the 'culture-gram,'" Steven replied.

We must have looked nonplussed by this answer, for a moment later Tim appeared next to our desk offering a sheet of paper. "Here's what it looks like," he said. He wanted to make sure we got a complete answer to our question. (The photocopied sheet Tim showed us was a "Culturgram [sic] for the 90s," produced by Brigham Young University's Center for International Studies.)

Later on we talked with Tim about being a special education student at Portage. We asked him whether his work with Daniel was very different from his regular classes.

"Not much," he said. "There's a lot less kids in Miss Daniel's class. There's only four first period, and four second period. In my other classes there's like twenty-five or something."

"So you get a lot more attention with Miss Daniel, right?" we asked.

"Same with the other classes, too!" said Tim.

"Really?"

"Yes. Mr. Bruns, my science teacher, is always walking around talking and everything."

"What did you hear about middle school before you got here?"

"That there was going to be drugs and violence and stuff. That it was bad. It's good, though. I think they're all full of baloney."

"If you got into some kind of trouble," we asked, "or you had some really bad problem, is there anybody here at school that you would be able to talk to about it?"

"Miss Daniel, Miss Clark, Mr. Bruns—all kinds of people. Miss McAbee, Miss Amborn, Miss Hudson, the counselor, Miss Bryant. . . ."

"Really? All your teachers? You trust them?"

"Yes."

"You'd be able to tell them something that you might be, you know, . . ."

"Unsecure in telling someone else? Yes."

"How do the other kids in this school treat you?"

"Like a regular kid."

"Anybody ever make fun of you or try and pick on you?"

"Yes. Trying to pick fights with me, but they don't pick on me because I have a learning disability."

Tim's mother reported a marked change in his attitude toward school after he came to Portage. "She doesn't have to force him to get out of bed and come to school any more," explained Daniel. "He's up before she is and heading for the bus. So numerous home problems, according to Mom, have dissipated with him being here."

Daniel works with children at all three grade levels, but she is considered a member of the sixth-grade team, follows their teaching schedule, and participates in all their team meetings and extracurricular activities. "That's worked out really well for me," she said, "and I think Chuck [Hoffman] is planning this coming school year to assign each of the other two special ed teachers to a different team. This faculty's really good about communicating. The seventh-grade team leader will come down and tell me if they're changing their schedule. The eighth-grade team leader does the same. I follow the progress of all my mainstreamed kids through weekly notes that we send out to the teachers with a small checklist with some room for comments."

We asked Daniel what she thought had contributed to Tim's improvement.

"Numerous things," she replied. "He's got a mom that really cares. They're real poor. Money's really tight and they're having a tough time. His natural father was an alcoholic, so he's coming from an alcoholic home (all nine of my kids come from alcoholic homes), but Tim's father is out of the picture now. So Mom's keeping as stable a home as she can, being a single mother with absolutely no money. He's happy here. He trusts everybody's judgment, and so he doesn't get upset when you suggest ways that he might be able to handle a situation better. He internalizes that really quickly.

"He had a problem this fall—he went on a school field trip and stole some things. I didn't go. I stayed with my other kids. So when the sixth-grade teachers told me that, Tim and I talked together about what would be the best way to take care of that problem, and he and I decided together that he would write a note of apology to all the teachers that had been sponsors of that trip. He wrote the note and then individually carried it to them and apologized. Some kids would have taken a belligerent, chip-on-the-shoulder attitude, but Tim really took it to heart. It did not become a blow-up situation for him. It never got to the level of being a formal disciplinary action. It was an isolated incident that was taken care of just between the teachers."

Tim's case illustrates the way a commonly cited advantage of teaming can be especially valuable for children with behavioral disorders. The close teamwork among the sixth-grade teachers at Portage enabled them to handle a situation, involving a major disciplinary infraction like theft, that in another school might easily have escalated into a crisis and seriously set back Tim's academic progress and social adjustment. It is vital in this story that the special education teacher is a full member of the team and therefore has the opportunity to act as an advocate for the student with all of his other teachers.

Teaming and Inclusion

The sixth-grade team's mutually agreed-on teaching style and classroom rules contribute to the success of mainstreamed students. For example, the fact that the teachers do not just stand in front of the room and lecture but as a matter of daily practice move around the classroom stopping at each student's desk for individual work means that students with disabilities do not stand out as unusual when they need special attention. Similarly, the teachers' strict enforcement of their team rule against making fun of other students means that Tim is less conspicuous as a student with disabilities. It's not that unusual for students in his classes to be reprimanded for making fun of others.

"If Tim's having trouble," Daniel said, "it doesn't look funny that a teacher stops at his desk and spends some time there, because he stops at every other desk, too. For the most part the teachers are real accepting of the kids, and I think that carries over to the other kids' attitudes. Tim doesn't get ridiculed much because he fits in. He's not very different. Some of my other kids who have serious psychiatric problems are pretty alienated. But that's their major problem; they don't know how to cope in society. That's why they're in my room."

Daniel is an experienced teacher who came to Portage after working in the Indianapolis and Warren Township public schools, at the Northeast Indiana Special Education Coop, and at Charter Beacon Hospital in Fort Wayne. She believes that the atmosphere at Portage is supportive of her students with disabilities in part because the general socioeconomic level of the students is low. There is less snobbery, she told us, less emphasis on outward appearances, and more acceptance of individual differences.

"This school is more accepting of my kids because they don't stand out as much," Daniel said. "We've got a lot of kids in the regular ed population that are coming in with lots of problems. They don't look a whole lot different from my kids. My kids normally have jeans that are a little too short and have some holes in them, and shirts that are faded over the years from too many washings. They don't have Nikes or Reeboks or whatever. In other schools that are more affluent, my kids have stuck out more and have been exposed to more ridicule."

"Does the staff here specifically try and foster an atmosphere where people are more accepting of each other?" we asked.

"I don't think they make a conscious decision to try to teach the other kids to do that," she replied. "It's just a daily example that the majority of the school is seeing from the majority of the teachers."

Relationships Drive the Change Process

Without question Portage Middle School could not have made such rapid and fundamental changes without the guidance of Principal Hoffman, and Hoffman in turn could not have been as effective without the thoughtful leadership and careful planning provided by the Fort Wayne Community Schools and especially Assistant Superintendent Sandy Todd. And Todd would certainly not have been able to accomplish all she did without the critical assistance and advice of Judy Johnston, the experienced MGIP technical assistance consultant from Pittsburgh.

In the other communities we looked at, the influence of the central office was either mixed or largely irrelevant. But in Todd, the Fort Wayne schools had a district administrator who exercised the kind of leadership that, in many other communities, was found primarily at the building level. And the strength of that leadership, as we have seen in the stories of the other schools in this book, came from the ability to nurture mutually respectful and honest personal relationships.

"Sandy was the driving force behind the change," said Johnston. "Part of it was the respect people had for her. She had an easygoing, supportive, facilitative way of working with the principals. But she had earned her stripes. They knew that she had been a principal herself and that she knew what she was talking about."

Todd knew that the transition to interdisciplinary teaming in Fort Wayne's middle schools was both central to the school improvement effort and also fraught with dangers. She created a central steering committee to guide the initial MGIP grant development process and met regularly with the middle school principals to set priorities and come up with an overall district strategy for change that made sense. Todd had the respect of the principals not just because of her experience but because she held the power of the purse: they knew she was responsible for making MGIP budget decisions.

Rather than have all eleven middle schools make the change at once, the committee decided to spread it out over a period of several years, with two or three schools making the transition each year. Scarce extra resources, staff positions, and professional development funds were rationed out to the schools making the switch to teaming in the years when they most critically needed them. If the money had been equally distributed among the eleven middle schools in Fort Wayne, its effect might well have been diminished.

Once the principals were actively engaged in the transition planning, Todd and Johnston were able to lean on them and insist that teachers be involved as well. "We told them that they had to have an instructional cabinet," said Johnston, "with teacher-leaders taking part in the planning for change. We used the issue of relationships—that the reason they felt engaged in the work was because Sandy engaged them. In just the same way, it couldn't just be the principal coming in and telling teachers they had to do all these things. We worked them over on the idea that once the teachers were involved in the planning they would bust their butts to make this thing work.

"The same thing was true for me, too," said Johnston. "I found that, over the years, I got more involved with the people there and I started to identify with their struggle. I wanted them to succeed."

After three years of experience under MGIP, Todd and Johnston decided to strengthen the program further by giving schools even more ownership of the change process. They began with a full-day planning session involving a teacher and principal from each school. This group agreed to focus on interdisciplinary instruction and multicultural education in future years, and these broad goals were written into the second-round proposal sent to the endowment. At the same time, the steering committee decided to set up an internal proposal process for schools within the district to request MGIP funds for their building. The process included a request for proposals, selection criteria, and a proposal review procedure. Participation in the MGIP effort was completely voluntary; if schools wanted to receive funds, however, they needed to complete the application process.

Eight of the eleven schools elected to submit a proposal during the first round of applications. Steering committee members critiqued each proposal, noting its strengths and weaknesses. They decided to accept three, reject three, and accept the others with reservations. During the second round, more proposals were received. This time, the committee decided not to reject any of the proposals but to allow schools to revise their proposals if necessary. The difference in quality between round one and two was significant. The process was repeated annually.

According to Todd, "This process added a whole new dimension to the Middle Grades Improvement Program in Fort Wayne.

Schools gained a deeper understanding of what they wanted to do and a greater sense of ownership. They knew what the change process was all about."

"We're Gonna Make Some Changes"

When we visited Portage in the spring of 1992, Chuck Hoffman was in his twenty-seventh year as a middle grades administrator. He is a tall, jovial man with a lot of laugh lines in his face, and he is a born storyteller. (Hoffman retired at the end of the 1992–93 school year and was succeeded as principal by Patricia Tharp.)

"I got transferred here to Portage on July 11, 1990," Hoffman told us, "and I sent the staff a letter on the fifteenth saying, 'We're gonna make some changes.' We used *Turning Points*, the Carnegie Report, basically. That's where we started. Then I designated my team leaders, and I started meeting with them on a weekly basis all summer. I knew that if I could get them fired up, then they would do my work for me. Because those are the people the teachers listen to. Whenever I come back from a conference with a new idea, they say, 'Ah, it's another damn dumb Hoffman idea.' But if another teacher says it, 'Wow!' They go for it.

"We started with some in-service on the characteristics of the early adolescent. I mean, we started from ground zero. We took a look at the Carnegie Report, and we did a staff evaluation of where we fit into that whole scheme and found out we weren't doing much. Portage was behind because they never did do the Middle Grades Assessment Program that was part of the initial phase of MGIP. It came in a contract year, there was a big slowdown on, and they decided not to participate. So they had never really done a comprehensive study. Well, they did a performance-based accreditation study, but that's nothing like doing the MGAP, which is the best thing that ever happened to any school."

Hoffman described the beginnings of middle school reform in Fort Wayne and the roles played by Sandy Todd and Larry Johnson, who went on to become principal of the highly regarded Kekionga Middle School, also in Fort Wayne. "We tried to do some things before MGIP," said Hoffman. "We converted from a 7–8–9 to a 6–7–8 grade structure. I was principal of the Fairfield School then. We went to meetings of the Michigan Middle School Association, which was one of the strongest in the country at that time. And we went down to Louisville, Kentucky, and visited some of the schools there.

"There were a few of us doing a few things. But we were using a shotgun approach. We had a few experts in to consult, but it was always just one shot. Nothing happened.

"It was about the third year after we converted to 6–7–8 that I had two teachers come to me, a math teacher and a social studies teacher, and they said, 'Chuck, give us a block of time with some kids. We'd like to do something with them.' Now that was just two teachers out of the entire staff, in a school of almost eleven hundred students.

"One of the English teachers got wind of it and said, 'Hey, they're doing some pretty neat things. Could I get involved in that?' That was the start of interdisciplinary teams in Fort Wayne. Before long we got some grade-level blocks going. Nothing like we have today, but at least we got some teachers working together, and then those teachers started talking to other teachers. So a lot of pressure came on the Fort Wayne Community Schools because none of the other schools were doing anything, and the teachers were talking to each other.

"About five years ago Sandy Todd came to us at one of our meetings—she was our director at that time—and she divided us into teams of three principals. She said, 'I want you guys to take a look at different types of scheduling.' I worked with two, and Larry Johnson, who was my assistant principal at the time, worked with two. Larry and I thought alike and did a lot of dabbling together.

"We started coming up with ideas, and the two principals that I met with kept saying, 'I can't do it in my school. I can't do it in my school.' And Larry had the same thing with his two. So Larry and I said, 'The hell with it. Let's you and I work together.' We put together an interdisciplinary schedule and presented it to Dr. Todd, and she tried to get us all the staffing she could.

"But we were still not making much progress with the business department and some other people that just didn't understand middle school scheduling. So Larry and I put together a two-and-a-half-hour presentation, with overlays and everything else. We went down and presented it to the director of personnel, the assistant director of personnel, all the business department, and the associate superintendent—where we started, what was wrong with the shotgun approach, what we had done, and why this type of schedule required more teachers. And it does.

"I was by then principal at Geyer Middle School, and Larry was at Kekionga. As a result of that presentation, the next year at Geyer I got a full staff and Larry got a full staff. Now it's really beginning to mushroom, see? And in the meantime we had brought in Elliot Merenbloom [an expert on middle school teaming and scheduling] to do some work with us. So now teachers were starting to say, 'Why can't we do what Geyer and Kekionga are doing?'

"When they transferred me here to Portage I felt that, since I'd been through it before, I could get this staff ready in one year. And we did. And I'm happy to say that next year two more schools will be going to interdisciplinary teams: Miami and Lane. And the following year we'll convert the last three."

Motivation: The Hoffman Prescription

"To me, being principal is 90 percent personality," said Hoffman, "and 10 percent knowledge. Because if you can get along with people—if you're a motivator of people—you can get them to do anything.

"So I spend a lot of time with my staff. I try to get to four or five team meetings every week. I just sit there as an observer. They'll ask me a question and I'll say, 'I don't know what you're talking about.' I'm not gonna answer their questions for them.

"You have to compliment people when they do a good job. And you have to compliment them when they don't do a good job, and then you have to talk to them. You have to be receptive to their ideas.

"The biggest drawback of interdisciplinary teams is that it does sort of segregate your school. You've got these grade-level teams and, boy, they're fired up for that grade level, and sometimes they lose perspective on what the other grades are doing. So it's important to have a lot of social events for them and to have different teams occasionally meet together.

"I try to motivate my staff to try something new even if they fall flat on their face. I don't know how some of these administrators and some of these teachers can do the same thing over and over and over, month after month, year after year. I'm not built that way. I just can't do that.

"There has to be some reason there for instilling change. I believe that if you don't have the energy at the top level in the building, just forget it. So I try to instill something, to try something new. Even if you fail, try something. Now that we have a schoolwide math-science emphasis, that's going to help to change the style of instruction, because the teachers have to work together.

"We worked on it up in Plattville, Wisconsin, at the interdisciplinary teaming conference that I took the sixth-grade team to last summer. We were told by our new superintendent that he wanted every building, every middle school, to offer a special curricular emphasis, because he believes in open enrollment and choice.

"The faculty was involved in making the decision to choose the math-science emphasis—especially the sixth-grade faculty, because they were the ones who had to do it first. We have three years to phase it in. I just got the sixth-grade team ten hours paid to do a formal evaluation. Because some of the activities were well accepted by the kids and some were not. We need to make changes. But the teachers are deciding along with the kids what changes will be made.

"One thing that bothers me is that we do not do enough follow-up in-service. It's one shot here, one shot there. But I think things are changing. When we got our first grant from Lilly, that's when things started pulling together, because we had some additional money. We had people sitting down and talking: 'I'm gonna use it this way. Can we combine our staffs to get a better bang for the buck?' and things like that. When we got our first grant, that is where things really started moving.

"That's when I got my team leaders and took them to Columbia, Maryland, and to Pittsburgh to visit the teacher training centers there. When you have an outstanding teacher who's been teaching for eighteen years and he comes up to you and says, 'Mr. Hoffman, this is the first perk I've had in eighteen years—the first time I've gone anyplace for a conference or anything of that sort,' that's when you get those people on your side. Then your job's easy.

"But we would never have had the money to do those things if it hadn't been for the Lilly grant. MGIP is making a tremendous impact. It's a slow process. When you take a look at Fort Wayne, we started out with no teams—well, I should say, with no school with what I would call a middle school philosophy, and come next fall we're going to have only three schools that aren't going to be at least part way there.

"Plus you've got some advocates of middle school education that keep a lot of pressure on downtown administration, too. There's a few of us banging their ears all the time."

Still More to Be Done

The "Culturgram" that was being used in Tim's social studies class as a source for a multicultural lesson was symptomatic of one of the unaddressed needs at Portage Middle School (and in classrooms at other MGIP schools as well). This dittoed sheet led students to do little more than recite facts in their oral reports: "Mexico has a lot of sports. The capital of Mexico is Mexico City. The average temperature is 75 degrees. Buses are a common form of transportation."

We did see many teachers at Portage beginning to use cooperative learning strategies, hands-on teaching activities, interdisciplinary instruction, and other practices well suited to young adolescents. But still evident was a heavy reliance on textbooks and worksheets and little use of multimodal materials and learning strategies. The teachers needed more help with learning how to use rich curricular materials; posing and encouraging students to pose meaningful questions; engaging students in stimulating and thought-provoking discussion; emphasizing depth over breadth of coverage; integrating reading, literature, and writing; and relating instruction to the personal lives of the students.

Hoffman emphasized the importance of having a student-centered staff in the middle grades and the important role of younger teachers in moving a more traditional staff in that direction. "Some of the older teachers here didn't want to change," he said. "They're slow in catching on to everything. They do a heck of a good job as far as the team structure is concerned, but to get them off this lecture, note-taking, regurgitation type thing is really a battle.

"I was able to add a few pretty good young teachers with some pretty good ideas," Hoffman told us. "This is going to be an advantage for middle-schoolers in the future, because there's a lot of us old folks getting about ready to hang it up. We need to get a good training program going for people that are excited about middle school.

"I talk to a lot of teacher groups and try to encourage them to get into middle school education. They say, 'Aaagh! I can remember when I was a middle school kid!' That's the reaction you get. Of course, they didn't know what they were doing back then. Everybody was floundering. That's what's fun about this."

An Uncertain Future

Ironically, two years after our visits to Fort Wayne in 1992, when the prospects for middle school reform looked so bright there, the picture has turned darker and more uncertain. Chuck Hoffman's fear that Superintendent Coats might not stick around turned out to be well founded, as Coats left Fort Wayne in 1994 to manage youth programs at the W. K. Kellogg Foundation. Even before his departure, a reorganization of the school administration designed to decentralize the system left Sandy Todd isolated from the middle schools she worked so hard to improve. And a major budget crunch in the spring of 1994 threatened to eliminate so many middle school teachers that Todd feared teaming would have to be abandoned at many or all of the eight schools that had embraced it so enthusiastically.

"In order to make teaming work we ended up adding thirty-five or forty teachers in the middle schools," said Todd. "That's a chunk of money. Now we have a different structure, with six area administrators making financial and staffing decisions. They weren't involved in any of the planning and thinking about underlying philosophy that led to the changes we made. Middle school doesn't seem to be a big priority at the moment."

In the two years following our visits, Todd reported, Fort Wayne's middle schools continued to make significant progress. "We have totally done away with tracking in middle schools throughout the system," she said, "and we made a real strong move last year toward inclusion. We have no pullouts anymore, and virtually all the kids with disabilities are in regular classes all the time. We're stressing the use of differentiated curricula and getting away from textbooks. That one's hard for a lot of teachers; it takes a total retraining. We've done a lot of curriculum development projects over the summer, and the teachers have done some great things."

Given the critical importance of the interdisciplinary team structure to every one of these positive changes in the schools, the prospect of seeing teaming dismantled was terribly discouraging for Todd. She took a few moments to reflect on how far the schools had come and on the most important elements of the process.

"If we hadn't had MGIP," she said, "we would never be where we are now. It put the focus squarely on the middle schools. There would never have been that much attention paid to them. The MGIP money stimulated us to look at the program. It got people excited to think that there was something to be done specifically for middle school kids. The staff development funds were crucial. It wasn't that much money, really, but it was enough to let the teachers know that they're important. It made them feel good about the job they're in—that others recognized that it's a very difficult job, and a very important one."

MGIP's technical assistance component was a critical factor in certain districts, and Fort Wayne was one of them. "My association with Judy Johnston worked beautifully," said Todd. "She became like a staff member. Over the years, as she came back to Fort Wayne again and again, she really got to know the schools, to establish personal relationships with the people, and they came to rely on her. It was a tremendous help.

"Judy stressed the value of data gathering and using statistical information to drive decisions—like with reducing suspensions. Having the data helped teachers to challenge their assumptions and to decide to do something about the problems. It got the teachers working together.

"MGIP personalized middle schools for us. You can see it in the sensitizing of teachers. Now they're thinking about the kids instead of just thinking about the subjects they teach."

Will the momentum created by seven years of successful middle school change in Fort Wayne be stopped by a budget crisis and a change of leadership at the top of the system? We know only that the answer will affect the well-being of thousands of young people and will bear watching by all who are interested in the long-term viability of systemic school reform.

Chapter Seven

Nine Essential Lessons

The four schools highlighted in this book were all part of the Middle Grades Improvement Program, sponsored by the Lilly Endowment. MGIP did not provide participating schools and school systems with a detailed blueprint for change. Rather, it offered a broad vision of middle school reform, seed money, technical assistance, and the freedom to choose local solutions to locally identified problems—a personalized approach to transformation.

MGIP has helped teachers and other educators see young adolescents with new eyes. It has also helped young adolescents view themselves in new ways. As a result, the conversation in participating school systems has changed, and a new vocabulary and vision of middle level education has emerged. Middle schools are no longer watered-down high schools. Over the years, participating schools and school systems have moved ever closer to the model middle school envisioned by leaders in the middle school reform movement.

Looking back over the program's history and progress, founder Joan Lipsitz said that "there is not a participating school I wouldn't prefer having my child in now rather than before." At the same time, Lipsitz wants to "catapult the schools to the next level." Technical assistance consultant Norm Newberg agreed. "Our work is unfinished," he said. "The distance is far off. Yet knowing the entry point, the image, and how you keep moving forward is important."

Within this overall context, what happened was highly variable. Many MGIP schools, like the four described in this book, made significant progress in school "restructuring." That is, they made fundamental changes in organization and management, school climate, students' learning experiences, the professional life of teachers, and school-community relationships (Newmann, 1993). Most of all, they made great strides in personalizing the middle school experience. Others made more modest changes.

MGIP schools followed many different paths in their efforts to bring about change. Taken together their experiences suggest nine important lessons for those interested in middle school reform or school restructuring in general. These lessons apply especially to urban middle schools, where "disadvantaged minority learners often face special student motivation barriers because of differences in their earlier experiences in and outside of schools" (Braddock and McPartland, 1993, p. 154).

The first six lessons, which speak primarily to middle school administrators and teachers, focus on the fundamental attributes of successful middle schools and what it takes to get from here to there. The last three lessons, which should be of special interest to policy makers and change agents, address the external factors that can facilitate the transformation process. Although each lesson is discussed separately, they are clearly interwoven. Indeed, a major finding from the MGIP experience is that change in one part of the system is likely to bring about change in the other parts as well.

Lesson 1: Changing Middle Schools Begins with Personalizing Adult-Child Relationships

"Urban middle-grades schools should be full of poets," writes Anne Lewis, "because they are special places brimming with pathos, problems, and potential" (1991, p. 11). Yet few urban middle schools turn out poets who can write like Harshman's Semorris Moore, Samantha Winks or Carlos Moore. Too few have teachers and administrators who are driven by a moral imperative to help *all* children achieve their highest aspirations regardless of their culture, language, socioeconomic status, or perceived ability.

Something must drive the change process. Poet and author Maya Angelou says that "teachers must be lovers" (1993). They must love, care for, and cherish all those in their charge. MGIP consultant Bill Kerewsky, a recognized leader in middle-level education, said "they must feel anger, a passion, a desire to change the status quo."

Whereas the endless waves of educational reform have introduced new "technologies" in the form of organizational or curricular changes, the Middle Grades Improvement Program aimed at the heart of the matter: understanding the developmental needs of young adolescents and translating these into sound educational practice. "The Middle Grades Improvement Program started with children and the treatment of children," said MGIP technical assistance coordinator Peter Buttenwieser, "not with governance and the treatment of systems." It grew out of Lipsitz's own research and professional experience, which focused on what humane schools look like and the nature of developmentally appropriate practice.

Humane schools begin by knowing children well and creating meaningful teacher-child relationships. Many observers feel that, given the typical assignment of 120 to 150 students, urban teachers cannot begin to know each child's strengths and needs or build strong bonds with their students. Yet the teachers described in this book demonstrate that such knowledge and relationships built on that knowledge are possible.

Strong teacher-student bonds do not come about without considerable effort, and often personal sacrifice, but they are within the grasp of ordinary mortals. And a variety of middle-level structures can support them: adviser-advisee programs, interdisciplinary teams, exploratory programs, school-community partnerships, and the like.

The middle schools featured here, and others in the MGIP Network, also understand the importance of setting high expectations for all students. Many have taken steps to reduce or eliminate tracking and include students with disabilities in regular classes wherever possible. They are working hard to provide all youngsters with rich and challenging curricula. By teaching symbolism and metaphor, hands-on science, and accelerated mathematics to all students, not just to those who are designated as "gifted and talented," they send a powerful message—through actions, not just words—that each child has value. By providing developmentally appropriate curricula and instruction that is sensitive to individual differences, they not only maximize students' success in school but also expand their options for the future.

MGIP schools are also gaining greater sensitivity to cultural differences. When we initially conducted our site visits, we found that these schools were not immune to the racial and cultural tensions simmering under the surface of schools all across the United States. In the last two years, teachers, administrators, and parents in South Bend, Wayne Township, and other MGIP communities have begun to examine their own and other cultures through a variety of awareness activities. In turn, they are beginning to ask tough questions about school policies and practices: Why are African American students disproportionately channeled into special education? How do racial, ethnic, gender, and socioeconomic differences influence school culture, staff attitudes and actions, curriculum and instruction, disciplinary practices, student assessment, and community participation?

In their recent book *The Self-Renewing School*, Joyce, Wolf, and Calhoun write, "The creation of equity is not just a matter of improving inner-city schools. It is a matter of orienting all our young citizens to the moral necessity of creating a society where all citizens work continuously to improve the lot of everyone" (1993, p. 81). It is ultimately on the level of personal relationships between adults and children that this sense of moral purpose is born and nurtured.

Lesson 2: Changing Middle Schools Requires Personalizing Adult Relationships

Educators often talk about the importance of creating a positive climate that is conducive to effective teaching and learning. There are many indicators of school climate: a safe and orderly atmosphere, a school building free of litter and graffiti, smiling faces, and active student engagement in their work. The MGIP experience suggests that creating a healthy climate for children begins by supporting healthy relationships among adults.

Such relationships are important for several reasons. First, they provide a safe environment for honest, open communication and risk taking. Second, they facilitate shared decision making, in which individuals not only have a voice but real choice. They lay the foundation for a true learning community, one in which teachers are willing to serve as peer coaches, collaborators, and critical friends. And they model the kind of cooperative learning and mutual respect that teachers expect of their students.

Each of the schools described in this book set about changing the "rules, roles and relationships" (Schlechty, 1990) among administrators, teachers, and parents. Beginning with the very first planning grant, MGIP schools created planning teams to carry out in-depth needs assessments, set priorities, and develop long-range action plans. These teams altered the governance structure of the participating middle schools, expanding the number of school and community people involved directly in decision making.

Informal relationships between administrators and teachers also changed dramatically, as they worked alongside one another to bring about change. Rather than making pronouncements from on high, successful administrators teased, prodded, praised, and invited teachers to join them in taking risks. A few teachers complained that their principals were abrogating their responsibility by delegating important decisions to them or that they were being pushed too hard. But most cherished their new-found freedom and the increased opportunities for experimentation.

In many MGIP schools, the introduction of teaming, study groups, and other collaborative structures also led to new relationships among teachers. Ongoing professional development became a norm. The result was a "literacy of thoughtfulness"—a process of making meaning and negotiating it with others. Rex Brown captures this spirit of cooperation well in *Schools of Thought:* "[Thoughtful] schools and districts are distinguished by a different kind of conversation, a style of conversation that builds community. Although disagreements exist, they are in the open and are the subject of intense and sustained inquiry and debate. [Thoughtful] . . . schools are symbolically rich places, where vivid and interesting conversations are taking place up and down the hierarchy. Adults are visibly engaged in inquiry, discovery, learning, collaborative problem solving, and critical thinking" (1991, p. 233).

Over time, the MGIP schools moved beyond thoughtful sharing of ideas to changes in practice. A recent paper from the Institute for Research on Learning describes the power of learning in such "communities of practice." United by common enterprise, people come to develop and share ways of doing things, ways of talking, beliefs, values—in short, practices—as a function of their joint involvement in mutual activity (Wenger, 1991).

Diane Zych, former MGIP coordinator in East Chicago, describes how this movement from new ideas to action occurred in her district:

> Teachers in the city's two middle schools were interested in moving to interdisciplinary teaming, but first they wanted to learn more about it. So, over a period of two-and-a-half years, they voluntarily attended workshops, seminars, and conferences. They visited classrooms and schools where teaming was being used. They viewed videos and were inundated with printed materials.

During that period we gained a number of converts and a still larger number of others willing to listen. What is crucially important is that teachers were given numerous and repeated opportunities to learn and to stretch professionally. Over time, pioneer team members began serving in a sense as researchers in on-site laboratories where they could demonstrate quite visibly the efficacy of the teaming process. Other teachers were encouraged to visit their classrooms and to ask very direct questions. Perhaps most important, they could witness in very concrete terms theory put into practice. (1991, p. 3)

Lesson 3: Changing Middle Schools Requires Transformational Leadership

The MGIP experience also makes clear the critical importance of transformational leaders in school restructuring (Smith and Andrews, 1989). What is transformational leadership? It draws people in to the process of making hard decisions and empowers those who participate in that process. It helps people redefine their purpose and vision, renew their commitment, and restructure their organizations in ways that help them accomplish their goals. In the most effective schools, there are many leaders, not one. In the four schools described in this book, principals and teachers played important roles in bringing about fundamental change.

Principal Leadership

The five principals featured in this book differed in a variety of ways, including personal style, gender, and culture. Despite these differences, all five were transformational leaders, driven by a moral imperative to meet the needs of poor, urban youth. They shared a number of other attributes as well.

All five principals had a clear vision for their school and used a variety of mechanisms to ensure that faculty members shared that vision. They spoke out at faculty meetings, wrote memos and newsletters, stuffed articles in teachers' mailboxes, and created professional development programs. Recognizing the importance of serving as role models and mentors, they made their values known through their daily interactions with staff and their ongoing evaluations of teacher performance. When new positions opened up, they were careful to recruit individuals whose philosophy and approach matched theirs.

Two of these leaders—Carlos Aballi and Wally Bourke—were new to middle-level education. They had to transform themselves before they could transform their schools, so they immersed themselves in the middle school literature, attended state and national conferences, visited other successful middle schools, and took advantage of each new opportunity for learning. Marcia Capuano, Jeff Swensson, and Chuck Hoffman were already middle school aficionados with years of experience in middle-level education. As MGIP unfolded, they became advocates and missionaries within their respective school systems, throughout Indiana, and beyond.

Transformational leaders solve problems in collaboration with teachers rather than alone (Leithwood and Steinbach, 1991). Group problem solving places individual problems in the larger perspective of the whole school. But to build collaborative work cultures, principals must concentrate on fostering vision and lifelong teacher development.

All five principals created standing MGIP committees whose purpose was to develop overall school plans and monitor progress, as well as ad hoc committees to address particular concerns. By involving representative groups in planning and shared decision making, they helped ensure that all members of the school community shared a common vision and understood the steps needed to get from here to there. In turn, a greater sense of ownership, empowerment, and efficacy permeated faculty and community members alike.

All five administrators were eager to experiment with new ideas, evaluate them, and make revisions when necessary. They were risk takers, willing to take on the central office, parents, or faculty members when it was in the best interests of their students and their school. When roadblocks appeared, they took detours, never losing sight of the ultimate goal. In the face of rigid bureaucracy, they followed the precept: "Act now, seek forgiveness later."

These leaders also recognized the importance of using data for decision making. They routinely examined school data—attendance, suspensions and expulsions, grades, and standardized test scores—to identify problems needing attention. When necessary, they broke down the numbers by race and gender in order to explore issues of equity and access.

As Fullan and Miles (1992) point out, "Change is resource hungry." In each of the schools described in this book, principals and other school leaders were entrepreneurial; they recognized the need for discretionary funds to promote change and took advantage of available funding opportunities. Even though most of the grants sought were quite small (generally from $1,000 to $15,000), they often served to stimulate teacher creativity, promote schoolwide planning, and encourage deeper innovation. With each new award, it became harder for these principals and their faculty to say, "If only we had the funds, we could do this or that." Rather, they asked, "How can we get additional funds to achieve this objective or initiate that program?"

Of critical importance, all five principals were highly accessible to staff, parents, and students alike. They rarely locked themselves away in their offices or spent precious school hours completing routine paperwork. They kept their doors open and were always in motion, roaming the hallways, observing teachers in their classrooms, participating in team meetings, communicating with students and their families, and getting out into the community. Through these activities, they got to know their staff, students, parents, and community members well, and they modeled the kinds of close relationships that they envisioned for teachers and students.

Teacher Leadership

Since not everyone is a born leader, the MGIP experience underscores the importance of carefully screening and training principals. It also argues for a system of checks and balances so that school reform is not entirely dependent on a single individual. Promoting teacher leadership is one such strategy.

MGIP fostered teacher leadership in a number of ways—for example, through teacher participation in school improvement committees, the awarding of teacher incentive (MGIP-X) grants, and the involvement of teachers in the MGIP Network. As a result, teachers grew and developed as individual practitioners, team members, peer coaches, and teacher trainers. A great many extended their activities beyond the classroom, serving as change agents in their own schools and providing guidance and support to colleagues across the state and the nation.

Like principal leadership, teacher leadership must be nourished. The MGIP experience suggests a number of factors that enhance teacher leadership: principals who provide a safe environment for risk taking, staff development programs that model active, inquiry-based learning for adults as well as children, and regular opportunities for both action and reflection.

One of the most powerful strategies for developing teacher leaders proved to be giving teachers the opportunity and support necessary to design their own interdisciplinary curriculum units. Developing such units provided teachers with a purpose for collaboration—one that went beyond talk to action. Furthermore, it encouraged teachers to think critically about what they taught and how, helped them break away from traditional disciplinary approaches, acknowledged their professionalism, and enabled them to share the products of their hard work with others.

Another highly effective strategy involved using teachers as trainers. Several MGIP school systems provided opportunities for teachers to train other teachers, as did the MGIP Network. These training opportunities served to acknowledge the trainers' growing expertise, while giving them the chance to share that expertise with others.

Lesson 4: Changing Middle Schools Requires Both Careful Planning and Ongoing Reflection

Fullan and Miles (1992) note that educational reform has been plagued by a steady stream of innovations such as cooperative learning, effective schools research, classroom management, peer coaching, and on and on. These innovations come and go, often without a trace. Such innovations are not organic; they do not grow out of the knowledge of the people who are supposed to implement them and who will be most affected by them. They are usually initiated in response to someone else's definition of the problem and the appropriate response.

In contrast, MGIP asked schools and school systems to take stock of their existing programs and look closely at how well they met the needs of young adolescents. The endowment also provided a considerable period of time for self-examination—from six months to a year or more. And it required that the planning process involve a broad array of people from both the school and the community.

Virtually all the MGIP schools used the Middle Grades Assessment Program (MGAP) to launch their school improvement effort (Dorman, 1985). MGAP had several benefits. First, it helped schools examine their practice in light of the needs of young adolescents. Second, by involving many staff and parents in data gathering, it encouraged ownership of the process and its results. Finally, it taught the importance of using data to guide decisions. Even after many years had passed, many of the teachers and administrators we interviewed felt that completing MGAP had been a critical first step in the transformation of their schools.

But initial planning is not enough. The four schools we studied routinely monitored their progress by tracking student data and convening regular meetings to discuss both accomplishments and continuing concerns. They also initiated more formal assessment procedures to evaluate the school improvement effort.

Teachers also need a chance to meet, plan, and reflect on what they are doing. This cannot be done in forty-five-minute faculty meetings or weekly planning sessions. Through block scheduling and other innovative approaches, schools found time for interdisciplinary teams to meet daily, schoolwide planning groups to convene regularly, and faculty to engage in ongoing professional renewal. During such meetings, administrators and teachers alike questioned where they were now, where they wanted to be, and what they needed to do to get there.

Lesson 5: Changing Middle Schools Requires Comprehensive Restructuring, Not Just Tinkering at the Edges

Fred Newmann, director of the Center on Organization and Restructuring of Schools, writes that systemic change focuses on all the main components of the system simultaneously (1993). A number of MGIP schools, like those featured here, introduced changes in virtually all aspects of the school program.

Most began by introducing organizational changes—creating new governance mechanisms that changed the nature of decision making within the school. In addition, they introduced other structural changes and programs designed to personalize the school experience: homeroom advisory programs, interdisciplinary teams, student assistance programs, and the like.

But these schools did not rely on structural change alone. They recognized that "new organizational structures may be necessary, but not sufficient to improve education" (Newmann, 1993, p. 6).

"The danger is that you can change structures without changing what happens to kids," explained MGIP consultant Aaron Fink. "You can change form without changing substance. For example, interdisciplinary teams can focus on discipline rather than on the curriculum or the needs of individual youngsters. Adviser-advisee programs can fail to change teacher-child relationships. And the availability of block scheduling does not necessarily affect how teachers use their instructional time."

The change process must touch what happens daily in schools. Unless restructuring efforts affect everyday routines—counseling practices, parent interactions, interactions between teachers and children—they are unlikely to have a lasting impact on educators or students.

Those schools that were most successful went beyond changes in organization and climate. As administrators and teachers became more aware of adolescents' academic needs, they began to introduce instructional programs that stressed learning by doing, application of knowledge and skills to real problems, and interaction with other students. They also developed interdisciplinary curriculum units on topics or themes that were not only socially significant but also highly relevant to the personal experiences, interests, and cultural traditions of their students. Finally, they worked hard to break down barriers among family, school, and community.

At their best, these program components were all interrelated. They were part of a shared vision, built on a solid understanding of developmentally appropriate practice for young adolescents. These schools focused "not just on structure, policy, and regulations but on deeper issues of the *culture* of the system" (Fullan and Miles, 1992, p. 751).

In some schools, the comprehensiveness of the MGIP program caused problems at first. In the early days of change at both Sarah Scott and Decatur Middle School, the number of innovations introduced simultaneously left many staff members confused and exhausted. It was only over time that faculty understanding, acceptance, and support for various innovations increased. Other schools, like Harshman and Portage, introduced several changes successfully in a relatively short time.

In the end, what appears to be of critical importance for successful school transformation is a keen sense of purpose and a clear set of priorities. Both slow, incremental change and more accelerated change can produce positive results, as long as schools keep their long-term goals firmly in mind.

Lesson 6: Changing Middle Schools Requires Establishing Close Links Among Home, School, and Community

Most elementary schools have a high level of parent involvement—parents belong to PTOs and PTAs, volunteer to run bake sales and help in the classroom, and turn out in droves on parent night. By the time youngsters reach the middle grades, however, parent involvement typically declines substantially. Many parents assume their children no longer want or need their active involvement once they reach early adolescence. Middle-level educators, in turn, often make little effort to involve parents in school affairs, while at the same time blaming them for their lack of interest.

According to researchers like Joan Lipsitz, home-school relationships are just as important at the middle level as at the elementary level if not more so. Young adolescents still look to parents for affection, guidance, values, and help with problem solving. Furthermore, strong parental and community involvement can help strengthen students' attachment to their schools and teachers for two reasons: "Children will often mirror the attitudes of the adults in their homes and neighborhood, and teachers may often show more personal interest in students when they know parents well" (Braddock and McPartland, 1993, p. 161).

The MGIP experience suggests that middle school parents are quite willing to become involved in their children's education when they have a definite role to play and are made to feel welcome. Most MGIP schools invited parents to serve as members of schoolwide planning teams. Others also created volunteer programs in which the roles and responsibilities of faculty and parents were clearly delineated.

In addition to these formal parent involvement efforts, MGIP schools used a variety of strategies to reach out to parents. Several created in-school parent centers—specially designated rooms for parent meetings and activities. Others assigned an individual, often a parent, to orchestrate parent activities. Many used social activities as the first step in bridging home and school. As James Comer points out, "By involving parents in the social climate, you create the trust that allows more parents to come in. Low-income parents are often people who didn't do well in school themselves and have bad memories of schools. You create activities that allow them to come in during good times—not just bad times" (1988, p. 5).

In addition to involving parents in their children's education, successful middle schools also strive to establish strong connections with groups, organizations, and individuals in the community. Such links are critically important for a number of reasons. First, young adolescents need the chance to explore their local communities in order to understand how they fit into them. Second, schools have never on their own been able to educate children or address their physical, emotional, or social needs. The family and outside social world have always been the primary influences on children. It is the recent breakdown of extended family and community support systems for many children that has placed them at risk and put educators under increasing pressure to do something about it. Finally, involving the community in the life of the school helps community members see both educators and students in a more positive light, which thereby increases public support.

Several MGIP schools worked in close collaboration with representatives of local business, industry, and higher education to develop career exploration programs aimed at expanding young adolescents' options. Others initiated community service projects that gave students an opportunity to participate meaningfully in the life of the community. Many established close ties with local health and mental health providers, social service agencies, and youth-serving organizations to better meet the needs of their students. Through such efforts the MGIP schools elicited both community involvement and support.

Lesson 7: District-Level Support Is Helpful but Not Essential for Change in Individual Schools and Classrooms

One of the greatest challenges for those involved in systemic school reform is determining the best point of intervention. Some view the school as the critical entry point; others focus on the school system; and still others (like Smith and O'Day, 1992) suggest that all layers of the educational system—classroom, school, district, state, and federal—must be fully aligned.

MGIP's creators have struggled with this issue since the program's inception. Although the endowment awarded planning and implementation grants to districts, much of the program's training and technical assistance efforts focused on individual schools. As a result, while many individual schools made significant strides, less than a third of the participating school districts succeeded in bringing about what might be called systemwide reform.

Lipsitz thinks the endowment may have inadvertently encouraged a "hands-off" policy at the district level. While she recognized the importance of systemic school change, she feared that insistence on strong central office support might have generated resistance in the beginning. So the program designers made a strategic decision to go to the schools because they felt there would be greater receptivity and success at that level. An unintended consequence was that most superintendents distanced themselves from the program until quite recently.

"One of the significant disappointments of MGIP," said Peter Buttenwieser, a consultant who helped design the initiative, "is that the program had far greater impact at the school level than the central office level. Unfortunately, we did not pay sufficient attention to the central administration early on. We should have used our store of goodwill to bring them along." In recent years, the MGIP Network has made a concerted effort to reach out to superintendents and other central office staff, and they have taken on a greater leadership role in the program.

What, then, is the role of district leadership in bringing about middle-level reform? The MGIP experience suggests that strong district leadership is highly desirable in effecting change across the schools in a system. When central office administrators understand the goals and objectives of middle-level reform and are committed to it, they are more likely to allocate needed resources and arrange for appropriate professional development activities. They are also less apt to transfer effective principals within two or three years, or to impose policies that undermine the change process.

District leadership involves more than the central office, however. School boards, teachers' unions, government officials, parent advocacy groups, and other members of the community can also facilitate or impede school reform. One way of bringing the various stakeholders in a community together is through creation of districtwide steering committees composed of district, community, and school representatives. In Fort Wayne, for example, formation of a broadly representative MGIP steering committee served as a powerful tool for change.

The MGIP experience also suggests that district leadership, while desirable, is not absolutely essential for change. Indeed, if district philosophy runs counter to middle school principles and/or district leadership is highly unstable, it may be helpful for district leaders to get out of the way. What seems essential in such cases is that some external authority—like the endowment, the MGIP Network, or a trusted technical assistance consultant—provide legitimacy and support for school reform.

Clearly, it is important to find the appropriate point of entry given the particular situation in a community and to build from there. As MGIP itself is about to enter a new phase, the endowment has adopted a two-pronged strategy for deepening and sustaining the change process. In four or five of the sixteen school systems, it will award "systemic change" grants, because these school systems seem to have the potential for strong district-level leadership. In the remaining school systems, the endowment will award "recognition grants" to individual schools that have demonstrated a commitment to change.

Lesson 8: Changing Middle Schools Requires Both External and Internal Change Agents

The MGIP experience suggests that outside intermediaries are an essential ingredient in the change process. Experienced change agents like the MGIP technical consultants can provide expertise, direction, an outside perspective, and support to those involved in the day-to-day realities of change. Yet external change agents cannot do the job themselves. To be effective, they must identify and build strong working relationships with internal change agents who can influence the process from within.

External Change Agents

For change to occur there must be a consensus that some things need changing. External change agents perform a critical function by helping create cognitive dissonance—a perceived discrepancy between what is and what should be. These outside intermediaries bring with them a new perspective, a vision of what is possible. They challenge educators to examine current practice in light of the latest theory, research, and craft knowledge. And they encourage educators to look closely at readily available data to see what is or is not working.

External change agents also perform a number of other functions: they serve as role models, advisers, mentors, and critical friends. Outside intermediaries can help school administrators and teachers manage local political controversies when they threaten the interests of students. They also help schools build on their strengths by honoring and celebrating their successes. All too often, those caught in the midst of change fail to see how far they have come; they tend to focus on how far they still need to go to reach their goal. Acknowledging small miracles—teachers engaged in higher levels of discourse, hard-to-reach parents becoming more active in school affairs, students excited about learning—helps validate the change process and encourages those involved to keep pushing.

The MGIP experience suggests that change agents are most effective when they are guided by an underlying set of values, know they have authority and are willing to exercise it, and stay the course over time. Effective change agents also know when to step back and when to press for change. Perhaps most important, they also recognize the critical importance of developing strong internal change agents who can influence the transformation process from the inside.

Internal Change Agents

Transforming middle schools requires more than limited or sporadic visits from outside intermediaries; the most successful MGIP sites also had strong district and/or school leaders who served as catalysts for change. For example, East Chicago, Fort Wayne, Indianapolis, Lawrence Township, and South Bend all had strong MGIP coordinators who worked hard to steer the MGIP program in the proper direction. These coordinators worked closely with individual school principals to create school action plans and develop comprehensive staff development programs to increase teachers' knowledge of young adolescents and improve classroom practice.

In the beginning, these internal change agents relied heavily on MGIP consultants, turning to them often for professional advice and support. Over time, they emerged as middle school leaders in their own right. Today, many of these MGIP coordinators, together with highly effective principals and teachers from the MGIP Network, serve as consultants to others in Indiana and beyond.

Lesson 9: Changing Middle Schools Requires a Multifaceted Intervention Strategy

There is a growing consensus that we need a systemic approach to educational reform (Smith and O'Day, 1992). The MGIP experience suggests that systemic change is highly complex, nonlinear, and influenced by a great many factors simultaneously. Those who seek to promote systemic reform would do well to use a multifaceted and highly personalized approach to change. Such an approach (1) is guided by a coherent framework; (2) incorporates "top-down," "bottom-up," and "sideways" intervention strategies; (3) is evolutionary in its design; and (4) recognizes that change takes sustained commitment.

A Coherent Framework

"It is essential to have a coherent framework when working in highly complex, interactive systems," said Lipsitz. MGIP provided that coherence. The emphasis on early adolescence—on research and experience with young people—helped adults see youngsters with new eyes, elevated the status of middle schools, and gave people in them new vision and a new vocabulary for middle-grades success. Despite the complexity of the MGIP design, this apparent simplicity was a distinct strength.

"Top-Down," "Bottom-Up," and "Sideways" Intervention Strategies

MGIP was the sum of various interconnected grants, not a predetermined grand design. Different entry points yielded different results in different schools and communities. The lesson for others engaged in systemic reform: using a multiplicity of strategies creates a critical mass of intensity, whereas isolated initiatives do not yield a momentum for change.

Initially, the endowment's primary intervention strategy consisted of "top-down" planning and implementation grants to school systems. In districts like Fort Wayne, these grants brought about impressive changes across the eleven middle schools in the system. Over time, MGIP added a number of "bottom-up" approaches aimed directly at school administrators and teachers: teacher incentive grants; staff development programs for school teams; and minigrant opportunities in reading, guidance, and the like. In many MGIP schools, these "bottom-up" intervention strategies served as the primary catalyst for change.

Not all of MGIP's intervention strategies were vertical, however. With the creation of the MGIP Network, the endowment also intervened "sideways"—that is, across sites. By involving district representatives in planning, providing opportunities for professionals to share with their colleagues, and promoting cross-site exchanges, the network helped create a shared vision and facilitated middle-level reform across the participating sites.

Evolutionary Design

Fullan and Miles tell us that "change is a journey, not a blueprint" (1992, p. 749). Like the school changes highlighted in this book, the MGIP design itself evolved over time. In Lipsitz's words, "It is an organic process based on emerging, felt, and observed needs."

Initially, the endowment gave MGIP participants considerable leeway in designing their own approach to change. The initial planning and implementation grants encouraged deep reflection and development of change strategies tied to local needs and concerns. After three years of grant making, however, endowment staff and consultants alike grew increasingly concerned about the slow pace and superficiality of the changes at many schools. To bring about real change, the endowment insisted that MGIP participants focus their efforts and provided them with additional incentives and supports to do so. Furthermore, the endowment issued a set of "nonnegotiables" designed to eliminate tracking, corporal punishment, and other harmful practices still in use.

Lipsitz likens MGIP to kudzu, the vine that runs wild in the South. Each new intervention strategy helped different people "see the light." Changes in participating schools and classrooms led in turn to changes in the MGIP design, which in turn triggered other changes at the local level. Over time, the middle school movement in Indiana spread well beyond MGIP. It grew to include a variety of other agencies and institutions—the Indiana Youth Institute, the State Department of Education, various teacher education institutions, and the Indiana Middle Level Education Association—each of which has become a stronger force for change (Mancini, 1993).

Sustained Commitment

Organizational development, like personal development, takes time. But all too often policy and grant makers allow only three to five years for a particular wave of reform to take hold. Such short-sightedness fails to take into account the fact that it took decades for us to develop the "factory model" of education that we have in place today (Fiske, 1991).

After nearly seven years, much still needs to be done to enrich classroom instruction and better meet the needs of all students in the MGIP effort, but the Lilly Endowment has stayed the course. As it enters Phase III, it is attempting to deepen and extend its past efforts, building on the strengths and shoring up the remaining weaknesses in its program design. Others who embark on systemic reform would do well to heed this lesson. Otherwise, we can expect many more waves of reform that produce little in the way of real and lasting change in practice.

A Vision of the Possible

The Middle Grades Improvement Program and the four schools described in this book suggest that fundamental transformation of urban middle schools is possible. It begins with a recognition of high moral purpose on the part of local teachers and administrators. Its bottom line is kids. Yet it requires effort on many different fronts and all levels of the education system—the classroom, the school, the school district, the community, and beyond.

Systemic change, like individual development, is fueled by personal relationships. MGIP was not only values driven; it was also personal in its design and implementation. At the local level, teachers built strong bonds with children, each other, and the administrative staff; and schools built new bridges to home and community. At the program level, the endowment encouraged personalization through every aspect of the program design.

By focusing on multiple sites within a given state, the endowment created a spirit of intimacy and camaraderie rarely found in the world of school reform. The sheer number and proximity of the participating sites helped create a shared vision, provided a strong impetus for change, and facilitated diffusion of new ideas throughout the program.

From MGIP's inception there were many avenues for close personal contact and support. Lipsitz and her colleagues at the endowment have provided consistent leadership and direction for the program. Their values and ideals have served as a beacon. Many of the MGIP consultants have also provided close personal support over long periods of time, with technical assistance coordinator Buttenwieser filling in the gaps. EDC has provided long-standing organizational support for both the technical assistance effort and various professional development initiatives as well. And, finally, with the creation of the MGIP Network, the endowment established yet another set of human bonds–teacher to teacher and administrator to administrator across the state.

The endowment also personalized the MGIP program in another way. It recognized that, although program sponsors can set a vision or direction, they cannot prescribe the shape of the change effort. Rather, each school, school district, and community must chart its own course. What sponsors can do, and the endowment did, is give all of the stakeholders—administrators, teachers, parents, community members, and students—the time and resources necessary to identify long-range goals and strategies for getting from here to there.

What we want for young adolescents is an expanded vision of their possible selves, along with the support necessary for making that vision a reality. We hope that, through these schools' stories, we have given urban middle schools a clearer vision of what is possible—even in poor neighborhoods with little in the way of special resources. And we hope that, through our description of the change process and the factors that facilitate or impede it, we have provided some support to those who are doing the essential work of making that vision a reality.

Appendix:
The Middle Grades
Improvement Program

What lies ahead is an exploration, and a highly
vigorous one. No one can predict where it will go or
what will be gained along the way. We feel certain
that it is a journey worth embarking upon and there
is every likelihood of both improving schools and
learning a lot while in transit.
                    —*Lilly Endowment Inc.* (1986, p. 9)

In spite of the urgent need for comprehensive middle school reform
and all that is known about adolescent development, few states or
school districts have attempted to change middle-level education
in a systematic way. One of the most significant efforts to date is the
Middle Grades Improvement Program (MGIP) in Indiana, initiated
in 1986 by the Lilly Endowment. Sixty-five schools in sixteen urban
school systems have received discretionary grants and technical
assistance from the program since its inception. The lessons of the
MGIP experience are essential knowledge for anyone embarking
on a plan for systemic school reform in the United States.

The endowment hoped to transform the very nature of urban
middle schools—their structure, the nature of curriculum and
instruction, and the relationships between teachers and children.
It used a number of strategies first to "jump start" and later to
deepen and extend the change process. The endowment's role pre-
sents an excellent case study of the scope and influence that can
be exercised on schools and school systems by thoughtful, powerful outside agents.

Initial Planning Grants

The initial noncompetitive planning grants were the foundation of the entire Middle Grades Improvement Program. To receive a grant, a district needed only to review the MGIP prospectus, attend an orientation session, and write a letter officially requesting support. According to Joan Lipsitz, the program's founder, the reason for keeping the application process simple was to "preclude the central office from 'planning' before the planning period. It was an attempt to ensure full participation during the planning process itself. The superintendents needed to agree to participatory planning toward a full proposal."

Nineteen of the twenty urban school districts that were invited to apply took advantage of these simple procedures, and all nineteen requests were approved. (One school system chose not to apply, primarily because it did not want any encumbrances placed on it.) Depending on its size, each district received from $15,000 to $25,000 to carry out a six-month planning effort. Since the endowment wanted each district to have adequate time and resources to rethink how its middle grades schools operated, in some cases it agreed to extend the time frame and provided incremental funding.

The planning grants had three key design features, all of which still undergird the MGIP initiative. First, the grants encouraged thoughtful reflection by applicants. Second, they required heavy involvement from both school and nonschool personnel. And, third, they encouraged "bottom-up" change tailored to the needs of individual schools and classrooms.

Thoughtful Reflection

The planning grants required districts to carry out intensive, thoughtful self-assessments—"to reflect on what exists and to invent something that might be better." The endowment asked applicants to respond to several probing questions: How was the planning team selected? How did the team come to know and assess the district's middle schools? Did it make site visits; interview students, teachers, and parents; or hold discussions with community members? How had the team's understanding of its middle schools deepened during the planning process?

To carry out their self-reflection, many schools used the Middle Grades Assessment Program (MGAP), a prepackaged method for evaluating the strengths and weaknesses of a school using exemplary middle school practices as benchmarks. Developed by Gayle Dorman while she was still at the Center for Early Adolescence, MGAP enlists parents, teachers, and administrators in examining all aspects of the school environment (Dorman, 1981). Six years after they had completed MGAP, many teachers and administrators still cited the assessment process as a critical first step in bringing about change.

Involvement of School and Nonschool Personnel in the Change Process

Another key feature of the planning process was the creation of partnerships between school districts and their communities. The endowment required applicants to bring together teams of people from their schools and communities to work on the plan. In many districts, teachers and administrators found themselves working with community members for the very first time. For some MGIP schools, the involvement of parents and community in the planning process led to profound changes in school-community relations.

For example, during the planning process, it became clear that parents at Northside Middle School in Muncie felt that their involvement and input were not wanted. The planning team decided to make parent involvement a high priority and sent several teacher teams to explore innovative programs throughout Indiana. As a result, Northside decided to develop a parent volunteer organization governed by parents, teachers, and administrators and staffed by a paid parent coordinator. In just one year, the school went from having virtually no parent involvement to having approximately 150 parent volunteers. Said Principal Chuck Childers, "The services provided by the parents have been unbelievable. . . . We now realize we had an untapped resource available for many years."

Bottom-Up Change

Although the planning grants went to school districts, MGIP's focus was on individual schools. The prospectus asked that schools look at every aspect of their organization and purpose, from how class schedules were created to how they engaged students in learning. This vision of bottom-up change inspired many different initiatives, including interdisciplinary approaches to instruction, smaller units for teaching and learning, enhanced student support services, and multicultural education.

While the emphasis on bottom-up change had a salutary effect on school-based change efforts, it had an unintended consequence as well. In too many cases, the central office at first took a back seat, which left program design and implementation entirely in the hands of the participating schools. As a result, individual schools made significant strides, but only about a third of the participating school systems took steps to bring about change in all the middle schools in the district. More recently, the superintendents have begun to meet as a group and take a more active role in the program.

Implementation Grants

After the planning process was completed, the endowment provided discretionary funds to those school districts whose implementation proposals demonstrated a strong commitment to bringing about fundamental change. The implementation grants gave districts the resources they needed to carry out their plans.

Phase I: Implementation Grants—The "Carrot"

From the beginning, the endowment recognized that even small discretionary grants can stimulate change. While the endowment has spent more than $6 million on the MGIP effort to date, the implementation grants awarded to each school system have been relatively small. For example, in the first round, each district received up to $150,000 over a three-year period, or $50,000 per year. Therefore, in districts with five or more schools, each school received less than $10,000 in seed money annually. Clearly, it was not the money alone but the opportunity to participate in a prestigious statewide program that was the catalyst for change. Like the planning grants, the first three-year implementation grants were noncompetitive. The endowment did, however, request detailed proposals that clearly linked program objectives, activities, and budget needs. It also insisted that applicants provide matching funds of their own.

Of the nineteen districts that received initial planning grants, sixteen ultimately received three-year implementation grants for fundamental school restructuring. "No one was rejected outright," according to consultant Peter Buttenwieser. Yet the stress, strain, and frustration of putting a program together prevented some from going on to the next round.

Districts could use their funds in a variety of ways—for needs assessments, staff development, conference attendance, site visits, planning meetings, consultants, new programs and activities, and the like. The endowment insisted, however, that applicants link their use of funds to a "driving sense of purpose" and outlined five priority areas from which they could choose at least two:

- School-based self-assessment and overall institutional reform
- Development of instructional leadership
- Enhancement of reading opportunities and instruction
- Dropout prevention and activities aimed at increasing

access to postsecondary education, particularly for the disadvantaged

- Building public support and a powerful "outside" constituency for middle-grades schools

With the exception of reading, the endowment asked districts to postpone major curricular reforms and focus largely on changes in organization and climate.

This approach seemed to work. Under the initial implementation grants, most of the MGIP schools made significant changes in their school organization and climate. They set up school improvement committees, focused on the developmental needs of young adolescents, improved student motivation, and strengthened adult-student relationships. Many schools instituted student incentive and reward programs, created advisory programs, enhanced student support services, and worked hard to strengthen links with parents and the community. All provided expanded opportunities for professional development, and many initiated creative reading programs as well.

Phase II: Implementation Grants— "The Carrot and the Stick"

After the first three years, the endowment faced a major decision. It could abandon the MGIP effort and move on to other programs or continue to fund participating districts. Recognizing that producing deep change in the way schools work with young adolescents requires a sustained commitment, it decided to provide support beyond year three, where it was warranted. These continuation funds became known as Phase II grants.

In order to inform their grant-making decisions, three individuals—Joan Lipsitz and Susie DeHart of the endowment, along with consultant Peter Buttenwieser—each visited several sites. Prior to their visits, they told the schools, "Show us what you are most proud of within MGIP, what you think you've done the best, and what matters most to you." While on-site, they gave the schools every opportunity to "strut their stuff."

The site visits revealed many impressive changes, from reduced absenteeism to improved climates for learning. Yet, the visits also highlighted the fact that many of the restructuring efforts were scattered and unfocused and several schools were still tinkering at the edges of reform. The visitors were dismayed to find continued evidence of corporal punishment, tracking, and use of suspensions and expulsions as disciplinary measures. In addition, the visits made clear that changes in school structure and climate had not automatically led to changes in curriculum and instruction. "There was greater understanding of 'whom we teach' and 'where we teach,'" said Lipsitz, "but not nearly enough change in 'how we teach' and almost none in 'what we teach.'"

Following these visits, the endowment invited school systems to submit proposals for extensions of their original MGIP grants. School districts could request up to $100,000 across two or three years, but the grants were not automatic. The endowment asked that sites "give even more careful thought to their proposals, lay out more ambitious realms of activity, and make an even stronger case for funding than they did in their original application." Schools could use funds to support new activities or strengthen successful ongoing activities but not merely to sustain and recycle what they had done before.

To focus schools' improvement efforts, the endowment asked that applicants *either* enhance instruction *or* connect the school with parents and the community, but not both. Lipsitz provided the endowment's rationale: "We felt that the districts and schools had shown that they couldn't do both. We wanted the program to extend the possible, not mandate the impossible. We learned, along with the grantees."

The endowment also insisted on three "nonnegotiables" designed to reduce or eliminate corporal punishment, tracking, and use of suspensions and expulsions to discipline students. These nonnegotiables caused a great deal of consternation among the MGIP districts, many of which felt tremendous resentment at being told what to do by an outside sponsor. Long-standing relationships between the endowment and key individuals in the participating sites were severely strained. In some districts, like East Chicago and Evansville, there was even talk of refusing to apply rather than submitting to such demands. Of particular concern was the call for the elimination of corporal punishment, a practice not only sanctioned by Indiana law but also written into most union contracts throughout the state.

In the end, none of the sites elected to pull out, and most of the tension between the endowment and the sites dissipated over time. Two years later, the endowment convened a group of respected teachers and administrators to obtain their views on the nonnegotiables and other MGIP strategies. To the surprise of Lipsitz and her colleagues, virtually all the site representatives present asserted that the nonnegotiables had been invaluable in bringing about much-needed changes.

When asked if he would recommend doing it all over again, Buttenwieser answered emphatically, "Yes. No doubt it initially set things back, but it was an important step forward. It gave people something to really deal with. While almost everyone said, 'We won't play,' they cared enough about the program to deal with it.

"The nonnegotiables were not about introducing new curricula or teaching styles but rather about the fundamental treatment of children," Buttenwieser added. "Foundations must have a value system and exercise integrity about it. How could you press for reform on the one hand and allow people to paddle kids on the other?"

Phase III: Implementation Grants— Selective Reinforcement

After the first two rounds of funding, the endowment elected to offer Phase III grants only to those school systems that had made a systemwide commitment to change. After consulting with But-tenwieser and the other technical assistance consultants, the endowment chose four school districts and invited them to apply for continuation funding: Lawrence Township, South Bend, Ander-son Community Schools, and East Chicago. A fifth district—the Indianapolis Public Schools—will continue to receive endowment funding through another grant program.

In addition to these systemwide grants, the endowment offered all sixty-five schools the chance to apply for recognition grants in the amount of $10,000 each. Twenty-six schools applied for such funding, and twelve received recognition grants, including Sarah Scott and Decatur and two schools in Fort Wayne. (Indianapolis schools were not eligible; they were funded separately.)

Technical Assistance

Beginning with the initial planning grants, the endowment decided to offer free technical assistance to those school systems that requested it. Thus, from the start, expert consultants have played a major role in promoting change at the district and school levels.

To ensure the success of the technical assistance component, Lipsitz asked Buttenwieser, the endowment's trusted adviser and consultant, to serve as coordinator. Buttenwieser selected the strongest individuals he could find, many of them seasoned veterans with many years of experience in educational administration and organizational change. Since there was little leadership capacity within the state at the outset, most of the consultants he identified were from the East Coast.

Buttenwieser assigned each consultant to work with one dis-trict, making an effort to match the site's needs with the consul-tant's expertise and working style. These early assignments launched a number of productive and long-lasting relationships. Technical assistance consultants formed strong bonds with local MGIP coordinators, principals, and teachers. As a result, they have succeeded in strengthening leadership capacity throughout the state. Many of their protegés have progressed to important leadership positions in their districts, while others have become leaders in the middle school reform movement both within Indiana and beyond.

In East Chicago, consultant Norm Newberg, a professor at the University of Pennsylvania, has helped bring about change at the district, school, and classroom levels. Working closely with the superintendent, he lobbied successfully to eliminate corporal punishment, urged that the district support more professional development, and helped promote strong leadership in the two middle schools. Newberg found a strong ally in former MGIP coordinator Diane Zych, now principal of one of the district's middle schools. Together they introduced teaming and advisory programs and fostered cooperative, inquiry-based, and interdisciplinary approaches to learning.

According to Newberg, changes such as these are just a part of the whole. They act "as exemplars pointing to fundamental changes in how teachers teach, how students learn, and how decisions are made." Newberg believes that "there is no single vision of a transformed middle school but rather many configurations that could be appropriate within a common value system." Furthermore, consultants do not have the luxury of demanding that existing schools restructure all at once. Rather, they must "figure out how to lead them in a direction that is more and more representative of the ideal [they] espouse."

George Silcott, an organizational consultant who works in both the public and private sectors, has been providing assistance to two Lawrence Township middle schools for nearly seven years. He serves as "adviser, listener, and challenger" to Superintendent Percy Clark, while serving as "enabler, supporter, trainer, questioner, and giver of information" to the principals and faculty of the middle schools.

Silcott helped Lawrence Township introduce teaming in all the middle grades—a move that required additional financial and staff resources from the central office. "These actions made a firm statement about the district's commitment to middle school philosophy," he said. "They put their money where their mouth was."

Aaron Fink, a former superintendent of schools in Massachusetts, has been a consultant for the Muncie Community Schools. Muncie had rejected outside assistance until after its initial implementation proposal was turned down. For the last several years, Fink has made a considerable difference in this school system, mentoring a new principal at Wilson Middle School and working closely with principal Chuck Childers to bring about improvements at Northside Middle School.

Fink encouraged Northside faculty to visit other middle schools and report back on their findings. Inspired by these visits, the school initiated the Teachers Training Teachers program, which has helped bring about changes in classroom instruction. With a somewhat embarrassed smile, Childers said, "I can't believe that we turned down such help at the beginning."

A few technical assistance consultants were not as successful, some providing too little assistance and others failing to meet local needs. Buttenwieser's philosophy was to select strong individuals and then give them plenty of latitude. "How they did their work was an individual matter," he said. "Yet they all had a profoundly clear understanding of the basic value system and beliefs of the entire group running the program."

Generally speaking, the most effective consultants were those with a deep knowledge of how schools and school systems work and a solid understanding of the evolutionary nature of change. Yet qualifications were not everything; there was also a matter of style. Two highly qualified consultants ruffled so many feathers with their tough questions and insistence on deeper change that their districts asked that they be replaced. Assigned to other sites, they were extremely well received and highly effective.

The consultants also met as a group once or twice a year, became resources for one another, and communicated regularly with

Buttenwieser. According to Lipsitz, the consultant meetings were important in shaping the program as a whole as well as the consultants' definitions of technical assistance. Looking back, however, Buttenwieser felt that coordination could have been stronger. "We could have pressed a little harder for a commonality of approach," he said, "and we could have made some changes a little faster."

MGIP-X Grants:
Encouraging Teacher Creativity

By January 1989, it had become clear that, despite significant improvements in school organization and climate, classroom instruction remained largely unchanged. Therefore, in addition to the Phase II grants, the endowment decided that MGIP needed some additional mechanisms for encouraging creativity in the teaching/learning exchange. One such strategy was formally entitled *Middle Grades Improvement Program: Strengthening the Instructional Process*. Known informally as MGIP-X (the X for extension), it consisted of small grants, in the range of $7,500 to $15,000, to "deepen the instructional process" in participating middle grades schools.

The first grants were for reading, writing, and language arts. The endowment asked that proposals address the heart of the instructional process, be relatively uncomplicated, and "developed by teachers for teachers." As with the earlier planning grants, the application process was simple, straightforward, and noncompetitive. Teachers could submit brief letter proposals, three to six pages long. The endowment promised to "look with particular favor on plans to immerse teachers in the creative process—and in discovery."

According to Lipsitz, the announcement for MGIP-X "struck a responsive chord among teachers, who understood that 'This one is for us.'" In fact, the endowment received so many applications that it ultimately issued three rounds of solicitations in the reading, writing, and language arts area, funding eighteen grants in all. The proposals were highly creative and individual. One, submitted by the language arts faculty at Anderson's South-Side Middle School, was entitled "Read and Feed." Developed with the help of Jack Humphrey, director of Indiana's Middle Grades Reading Improvement Program, the proposal invited teachers to explore young adult fiction extensively and to discuss their reading and teaching methods at a series of dinner seminars. The program represented an effort to break away from the text-book-oriented curriculum and establish a regular forum for teach-ers to exchange their ideas and practices. Several years later, these "Read and Feed" seminars are still going strong. SouthSide teacher Karen Sipes asserted, "There are layers and layers of spillover. These grants have been extremely effective in bringing about change."

A second round of minigrants encouraged teachers to link social studies and the arts. The endowment funded a total of nine-teen grants in this round, issuing two different calls for proposals.

One of these minigrants, entitled "From Pilgrims to the Pre-sent: A Travel Through Time," went to Anderson's EastSide Mid-dle School. Designed to link social studies, music, and art, the program involved more than two hundred students, along with sev-eral teachers and parents. Participating students carried out research on significant themes in U.S. history and developed an ambitious multimedia production under the direction of Sue Fin-ger, the school's award-winning music teacher. At the culmination of the unit, students gave seven performances to hundreds of elementary school children, parents, and community members. "The MGIP-X project was the highlight of my teaching career," said Max Perry, an EastSide teacher for twenty-two years.

Another grant in this round went to Geyer Middle School in Fort Wayne, which proposed involving the entire school in an interdisciplinary curriculum on the theme "the house." Students studied the architectural, social, and cultural significance of hous-ing through the ages, bringing in experts from the community. In a culminating activity, teachers turned the school's enclosed courtyard into an international village and teaching amphitheater.

A third round of grants focused on science, mathematics, and related technology. The endowment's Susie DeHart urged the endowment to issue this round of grants, citing the energy generated by earlier MGIP-X initiatives. As in earlier cycles, she counseled proposal writers about the endowment's goals and expectations and provided a much-needed human touch to the grants process.

In this round, the endowment received fifteen proposals and funded fourteen, many of which were also quite creative. For example, science and mathematics teachers at East Chicago's WestSide and Block Junior High Schools proposed to immerse seventh-grade students in an ecological investigation of East Chicago. Participating students studied the effects of industry on air, soil, and water quality; mapped the geographical features of the community; conducted population studies of the area; and began a recycling and energy conservation program.

The minigrants encouraged greater collaboration among teachers, helped link the disciplines, fostered innovative classroom practices, and promoted community involvement. The response from the sites was overwhelmingly positive. Mary Pat Hatcher-Disler, MGIP coordinator for South Bend, stated, "The MGIP-X grants helped teachers make connections, get involved, reach out, and continue the movement for change. Many MGIP-X teachers have become movers and shakers." According to Lucinda McCord, principal of Anderson's EastSide Middle School, "These grants help lure people out of the trenches."

There were some pitfalls. For example, some teams became so caught up in designing program activities—the "how" of instruction—that they paid little attention to "what" they were trying to teach. Other teams undertook such large-scale, all-consuming projects that they were reluctant to repeat them with other students in subsequent years.

According to Roberta Bowers, the former MGIP coordinator for IPS, some MGIP-X teachers might have benefited from additional technical assistance. "I would recommend proposal development help for teacher leaders," she said. "Some teams needed support in taking their ideas from the talking stage to the paper stage, while others could have used extra help in putting their ideas into practice."

The Role of EDC

In the spring of 1990, the endowment recognized that too many teachers were still relying heavily on textbooks and lectures to impart knowledge rather than helping students become active, independent learners. Therefore, in addition to awarding MGIP-X grants to teacher teams, the endowment decided to engage Education Development Center, Inc. (EDC) to work with a few school systems intensively to "deepen instruction."

A nonprofit research and development organization located in Newton, Massachusetts, EDC had a long track record in curriculum design, professional development, and school reform. According to Lipsitz, using EDC "was part of a concerted effort to strengthen intermediary organizations that serve as a vital link between the research and practice communities." By encouraging EDC to focus its efforts on the middle level, Lipsitz hoped to "generate sustained assistance for curriculum development and institutional reform."

To help bring about change in classroom practice, EDC introduced "Make It Happen!" to teams of teachers from school systems across the state. Make It Happen! is a well-tested approach to curriculum design that helps teacher teams design and implement active, inquiry-based curriculum units that link two or more disciplines. To date, more than sixty teams, consisting of two to five teachers per team, have participated in this professional development effort throughout the state of Indiana.

Indianapolis was one of the first school systems to participate in the Make It Happen! effort. Beginning in the spring of 1990, EDC worked intensively with a number of Indianapolis teams to design and implement thematic units spanning language arts, social studies, science, mathematics, and/or the arts. Following an introductory workshop, approximately thirty teachers from several middle schools volunteered to serve as "pioneer teams." They attended a week-long summer institute in Indianapolis where they worked together to create their units. Specialists such as librarians and program directors received additional training, so that they could serve as on-site facilitators throughout the school year.

That fall, some pioneer teams fine-tuned their curriculum units, while others introduced them in their classrooms. In May, the pioneer teams held a showcase conference at which they displayed their newly developed units to middle school teachers from across the district and beyond. The units encompassed many themes, from "Native Americans: The First Environmentalists" to "The Science Fact in Science Fiction." The showcase conference sparked interest among nonparticipating teachers and led to a second curriculum design institute in the summer of 1992.

With EDC's help, innovative interdisciplinary units have also become part of the curriculum in East Chicago, Anderson, South Bend, Evansville, Lawrence Township, Wayne Township, and other MGIP communities. For example, teachers at McGary Middle School in Evansville developed a program called LORE (Life on the Ohio River in Evansville) that links science, mathematics, history, and language arts. After researching the history of an old pagoda at the river's edge, students designed and presented a play delineating its role in the city's history. The production sparked the community's interest in refurbishing the decaying landmark.

In East Chicago, a pioneer team developed and implemented a unit entitled "We Are a Family." Each cooperative learning group formed a "family" with its own background and history that served as a source for creative writing. Another East Chicago team, composed of a language arts and social studies teacher, developed a unit entitled "American Adolescence," in which students compared the historical and developmental stages of early American history with the developmental stages of early adolescence.

EDC also helped launch two other MGIP initiatives aimed at improving equity and access for all students: (1) valuing diversity, a multicultural approach to education, and (2) inclusion of students with disabilities in the regular education program. In both cases, EDC worked closely with the MGIP Network.

The MGIP Network

The MGIP Network was created in the fall of 1989, when the sixteen participating districts were in either their second or third year of implementation. Individual schools and districts had made significant changes, but there was little cross-site sharing and little opportunity for schools to learn from one another.

The network had several objectives: (1) to provide MGIP sites with information on early adolescence, successful programs, and school reform; (2) sponsor joint professional development activities; (3) promote close, effective communication among sites; and (4) enhance collaboration with other national, state, and local institutions dedicated to young people.

According to Lipsitz, the network was an important part of the MGIP design. She said, "Over time it became apparent that program coordination needed to be moved out of my office if MGIP was to mature and persist." Since its creation, the network has become a vital mechanism for ensuring MGIP's continued growth and development. By integrating individual initiatives, it helped strengthen the program as a whole.

Hosted by and housed in the Metropolitan School District of Lawrence Township, located just northeast of downtown Indianapolis, the network is governed by a thirty-two-member steering committee—two representatives per MGIP site. One of these members is the site coordinator; the other is either a school administrator or teacher. Steering committee members help identify common needs, foster communication, and provide leadership for middle-level reform in Indiana and beyond. An executive committee, elected by the steering committee members, works closely with the network director in coordinating and monitoring the network's efforts.

During its first two years, the network carried out a variety of activities under the leadership of Director Barbara Jackson who had previously served as the MGIP community resources coordinator in Lawrence Township. Jackson hoped that the network would help MGIP schools see themselves as "part of a larger movement and part of a greater vision . . . furthering their sense of being on a mission with other committed peers."

The network published guides and resource packets on topics of common interest, developed a resource directory of middle school experts, sponsored a number of professional development activities, and arranged for school teams to visit one another. According to Jackson, these cross-site visitations "showed those who were embarking on change what was possible, while confirming for those already engaged in change what we're doing is right." They also helped empower teachers by giving them an opportunity to be perceived as experts by their peers.

During these early years, the network steering committee identified four major priorities for action. The first priority area was teaming. To encourage sites to institute interdisciplinary teams, the network identified effective teams across the state, scheduled cross-site visits for teachers, prepared resource packets, arranged for training events with national experts like Elliot Merenbloom and Nancy Doda, ran team-building workshops, and arranged for principals and teachers from one school to serve as guest speakers and discussants at another.

This multifaceted strategy paid off. Within a year or so, almost every MGIP school district had either created one or more pioneer teams, expanded teaming throughout the school, or developed plans to introduce teaming in the future. Although it is hard to attribute the introduction of teaming to any one individual or group, the network clearly brought the issue to the fore and provided strong technical support to those seeking assistance.

The second priority area was enriching classroom instruction. Together with EDC, the network cosponsored conferences for teachers and administrators designed to promote active, inquiry-based teaching and learning. By helping shape conference agendas and coordinating conference logistics, the network encouraged a feeling of ownership and shared responsibility for the conferences' success. Over time, the need for cross-site sharing grew, and the network arranged a number of regional meetings. These meetings, which were planned by teachers for teachers, came to be called "TNTs," for Teacher Networking Time. Highly popular, they gave teachers additional time to discuss their accomplishments as well as their continuing struggles in introducing classroom change.

Enhancing school leadership was the third network priority. To achieve this goal, members of the executive committee planned a Principals' Retreat for February 1991. Like its counterpart, the TNT, the Principals' Retreat was developed by principals for principals. Virtually every MGIP school was represented at the one-and-a-half-day conference, where participants had a chance to learn about the latest research on middle-level education and meet formally and informally with their peers. The retreat created many lasting relationships, which thereby reduced principals' sense of isolation. Away from the day-to-day demands of running their schools, they could reflect on their accomplishments, share their frustrations, give and receive advice from their colleagues, and, above all, learn that their problems were not unique. The first session was so successful that the Principals' Retreat has become an annual network event.

The final network priority, multicultural education, grew out of the concerns of several MGIP communities. At the sites' request, Director Jackson invited staff from EDC's Center for

Equity and Cultural Diversity to design a professional development program tailored to the communities' needs. Working closely with the network, EDC developed a series of institutes entitled "Valuing Diversity, a Multicultural Infusion Model."

Teams from all but four of the MGIP districts have now participated in one of these institutes. Those who participated learned that multicultural education does not refer merely to studying other cultures but rather to infusing a multicultural perspective into all aspects of schooling: school disciplinary and grouping policies, the formal and "hidden" curriculum, teaching styles, instructional materials, and community participation. By the end of each institute, participating teams had defined their vision of multicultural education, created a mission statement for their team, and developed an action plan for continuing this work over the next few years.

To deepen and extend the learning from the first round of institutes, EDC designed and conducted a "Diversity II Workshop" in close coordination with the MGIP Network. This second institute provided participants with an opportunity to explore issues of particular interest in greater depth.

These statewide initiatives have begun to bear fruit. Individual school teams have examined teacher-student interactions for gender and race bias, designed new curriculum units that address different cultures, revised their disciplinary policies, explored their local neighborhoods, and looked to see whether certain groups are overrepresented in special education. In addition, two school systems—South Bend and Wayne Township—have developed systemwide plans for infusing multiculturalism into their kindergarten through grade 12 program.

In recent years, the MGIP network has taken additional steps to become a force for change. To increase local ownership, it has established a number of working committees composed of MGIP coordinators, district and school administrators, and classroom teachers. To help shape state-level policy, the network has convened meetings with the MGIP superintendents and developed close ties to other groups and organizations, including the Department of Education, the Indiana Middle Level Education Association, the Indiana Higher Education Network for Middle Level Educators, and the Indiana Youth Institute. The network has also sharpened its focus, placing particular emphasis on those students who are most at risk.

Recently, the network launched a new minigrants program designed to facilitate change at the building level. To receive funding, applicants must show how they plan to mainstream students with disabilities and provide rich curriculum opportunities for all. According to Jackson, these grants are an investment in the future, helping to train "a cadre of committed professionals who can advocate for continued reform and serve as resources to others."

Said Lipsitz, "What is so exciting about the network's activities is that they are entirely voluntary. Not only do the participants not have to participate as a condition of their MGIP grant, but the network itself does not have to do these specific things. It truly is *professional* development."

Conclusion

Those who strive to create a national, regional, state, or local reform effort can learn much from the MGIP initiative. Clearly, the planning and implementation grants were essential. Despite their relatively small size, they were catalysts for reform. When well matched with local needs, the technical assistance consultants were also a strong force for change. By adding minigrants for teachers and professional development activities, the endowment encouraged schools to move beyond changes in structure and climate and initiate changes in curriculum and instruction. And, although sites strongly resisted them at first, the nonnegotiables eventually succeeded in reducing, and in some cases eliminating, long-standing harmful practices.

The creation of the MGIP Network was also a valuable change strategy designed to build on and strengthen all that had gone before. Through participation in the network, MGIP sites began to develop a common vision of what was possible. Members not only learned from one another but also grew professionally. Now, a new cadre of leadership has emerged within the state, one that can help sustain the middle school reform movement over time.

The MGIP experience also underscores the importance of gaining strong central office and board support for middle school reform. Without strong support at the district level, school restructuring efforts can become overly dependent on the leadership abilities of principals and their staff. While individual school change is important, changing large numbers of schools within a system requires a comprehensive, carefully coordinated approach.

Finally, those who embark upon systemic change efforts should, like Lilly Endowment Inc., be prepared to stay the course. Fundamental change takes time, and changes in structure and climate often precede changes in classroom instruction. Furthermore, in designing systemic reform efforts, program designers must build in flexibility, take periodic readings of sites' efforts, and respond to changing circumstances. They would do well to heed Fullan and Miles's (1992, p. 749) assertion: "Change is a journey, not a blueprint."

References

Angelou, M. "A Morning with Maya Angelou." Presentation at the Association for Supervision and Curriculum Development Annual Meeting, Washington, D.C., April 1993.

Beane, J. *A Middle School Curriculum: From Rhetoric to Reality.* Columbus, OH: National Middle School Association, 1990.

Benson, P., Williams, D., and Johnson, A. *The Quicksilver Years: The Hopes and Fears of Early Adolescents.* New York: Harper & Row, 1987.

Boateng, F. "Combatting Demulturalization." In K. Lomotey (ed.), *Going to School.* New York: Albany State University of New York Press, 1990.

Braddock, J. H., and McPartland, J. M. "Education of Early Adolescents." *Review of Research in Education*, 1993, 19, 135–170.

Brown, R. *Schools of Thought.* San Francisco: Jossey-Bass, 1991.

Carnegie Corporation. *Turning Points: Preparing American Youth for the 21st Century.* Washington, D.C.: Carnegie Council on Adolescent Development, 1989.

Carnegie Corporation. *Abridged Version of Turning Points: Preparing American Youth for the 21st Century.* Washington, D.C.: Carnegie Council on Adolescent Development, 1990.

Celis, W. "Educators Focus on the Forgotten Years: The Middle Grades." *New York Times*, June 10, 1992, p. B8.

Chira, S. "Harlem's Witness for the Chancellor." *New York Times*, August 10, 1992, p. B3.

Comer, J. "School-Parent Relationships That Work: An Interview with James Comer." *Harvard Education Letter*, 1988, 4(6), 4–6.

Darling-Hammond, L. "Building Learner-Centered Schools: Developing Professional Capacity, Policy, and Political Consensus." In J. A. Banks, L. Darling-Hammond, and M. Greene (eds.), *Building Learner-Centered Schools: Three Perspectives.* New York: Columbia Teachers College Press, 1992.

Dorman, G. *Middle Grades Assessment Program.* Carrboro, N.C.: Center for Early Adolescence, 1981.

Dorman, G. *Improving Middle Grade Schools: A Framework for Action.* Carrboro, N.C.: Center for Early Adolescence, 1987.

Epstein, J. L. "Effective Schools or Effective Students: Dealing with Adversity." In R. Haskins and D. MacRae (eds.), *Policies for America's Public Schools.* Norwood, N.J.: Ablex, 1988.

Fiske, E. B. *Smart Schools, Smart Kids: Why Do Some Schools Work?* New York: Simon & Schuster, 1991.

Fullan, M. G., and Miles, M. B. "Getting Reform Right: What Works and What Doesn't." *Phi Delta Kappan,* 1992, *73*(10), 745–752.

George, P. and Alexander, W. *The Exemplary Middle School.* (2nd ed.) Orlando: Holt, Rinehart & Winston, 1993.

Hawkins, D. Speech given at the National Prevention Conference, Federal Center for Substance Abuse Prevention, Washington, D.C., Feb. 1993.

Haynes, N. M. "Toward an Understanding of Personalization in Atlas Learning Communities." Yale University School Development Program, unpublished paper, March 14, 1994.

Hill, J. P. *Understanding Early Adolescence: A Framework.* Carrboro, N.C.: Center for Early Adolescence, 1980.

Holmes Group. *Tomorrow's Schools: Principles for the Design of Professional Development Schools.* East Lansing: Michigan State University, 1990.

Ianni, F. A. J. "Providing a Structure for Adolescent Development." *Phi Delta Kappan,* 1989, *70,* 673–682.

Joyce, B., Wolf, J., and Calhoun, E. *The Self-Renewing School.* Alexandria, Va.: Association for Supervision and Curriculum Development, 1993.

Kandel, D., and Lesser, G. *Youth in Two Worlds.* San Francisco: Jossey-Bass, 1972.

Kozol, J. *Savage Inequalities: Children in America's Schools.* New York: Crown, 1991.

Leithwood, K. A. "The Move Toward Transformational Leadership." *Educational Leadership,* 1991, *49*(5), 8–12.

Leithwood, K. A., and Steinbach, R. "Indicators of Transformational Leadership in the Everyday Problem Solving of School Administrators." *Journal of Personnel Evaluation in Education,* 1991, *4*(3), 221–244.

Levin, H. M. "Accelerated Schools for Disadvantaged Students." *Educational Leadership,* 1987, *44*(3), 19–21.

Levy, S. Presentation to the Association of Experiential Education, October 1993.

Lewis, A. C. "Gaining Ground: The Highs and Lows of Urban Middle School Reform." New York: Edna McConnell Clark Foundation, 1991.

Lilly Endowment Inc. *Middle Grades Improvement Program: Prospectus.* Indianapolis: Author, 1986.

Lipsitz, J. *Growing Up Forgotten*. Lexington, Mass.: Heath, 1977.

Lipsitz, J. *Successful Schools for Young Adolescents*. New Brunswick, N.J.: Transaction, 1984.

Mancini, G. *Gentle Ambitions: Indiana's Thoughtful Middle Grades Movement*. Washington, D.C.: Education Writers Association, 1993.

Mitchell, J. J. *Adolescent Psychology*. Toronto: Holt, Rinehart & Winston, 1979.

National Middle School Association. *This We Believe*. Columbus, OH: Author, 1982.

Newmann, F. M. "Beyond Common Sense in Educational Restructuring: The Issues of Content and Linkage." *Educational Researcher*, 1993, 22(2), 4–22.

Oakes, J. *Keeping Track: How Schools Structure Inequality*. New Haven, Conn.: Yale University Press, 1985.

Piaget, J. *The Essential Piaget*. New York: Basic Books, 1977.

Schlechty, P. C. *Schools for the 21st Century: Leadership Imperatives for Educational Reform*. San Francisco: Jossey-Bass, 1990.

Sizer, T. *Horace's School: Redesigning the American High School*. New York: Houghton Mifflin, 1992.

Smith, W. F., and Andrews, R. L. *Instructional Leadership: How Principals Make a Difference*. Alexandria, Va.: Association for Supervision and Curriculum Development, 1989.

Smith, M., and O'Day, J. "Systemic school reform." In S. Fuhrman and B. Malen (eds.), *The Politics of Curriculum and Testing*. Bristol, U.K.: Falmer, 1992.

Sorenson, R. *Adolescent Sexuality in Contemporary America*. New York: World, 1973.

Stevenson, C. *Teaching 10–14 Year Olds*. New York: Longman, 1992.

Van Hoose, J., and Strahan, D. *Young Adolescent Development and School Practices: Promoting Harmony*. Columbus, Ohio: National Middle School Association, 1988.

Wenger, E. "Communities of Practice: Where Learning Happens." *Benchmark*, Fall 1991, pp. 6–8.

Wheelock, A. *Crossing the Tracks: How "Untracking" Can Save America's Schools*. New York: New Press, 1992.

Wheelock, A., and Dorman, G. *Before It's Too Late: Dropout Prevention in the Middle Schools*. Boston: Massachusetts Advocacy Center, 1988.

Wiles, J., and Bondi, J. *Making Middle Schools Work*. Alexandria, Va.: Association for Supervision and Curriculum Development, 1986.

Zych, D. *School City of East Chicago*. MGIP Interim Report, Period: July 1, 1991–December 31, 1991.

Index